Hopkins

The work of
Michael Hopkins
and Partners

Colin Davies
with essays by
Patrick Hodgkinson
and Kenneth Frampton

Hopkins

The work of
Michael Hopkins
and Partners

Phaidon Press Limited
140 Kensington Church Street
London W8 4BN

First published 1993
© 1993 Phaidon Press Limited

'An English Sensibility: the making
of an architectural technology'
© 1993 Patrick Hodgkinson

ISBN 0 7148 2782 7

A CIP catalogue record for this book
is available from the British Library

Printed in Hong Kong

Photography credits
(l) left, (r) right, (t) top,
(m) middle, (b) bottom

Alinari, Florence p166
Architectural Association pp164(r),
165(r)
David Begg p56
Tim Benton p235(r)
Dave Bower pp17, 50(t), 53(t), 58,
64–5, 74, 78–87, 90, 94, 96, 98, 167(l)
Richard Bryant/Arcaid pp14, 48,
50(b), 53(b), 88, 92(l), (100)
Canopy p143(t)
Martin Charles pp19, 23(l), 92(r),
95, 101–9, 113, 123, 126, 133,
136, 149–51, 154–5, 157, 160–1,

164(l), 167(r), 169(r), 171
Peter Cook pp120–2, 124,
128–9, 235(t)
Richard Davies pp6, 24(r), 25(l),
172–6, 178–229, 232(b)
Alan Delaney/Wordsearch pp152,
156
Richard Einzig/Arcaid p9
Stephen Games/Architectural
Association p232(tr)
Dennis Gilbert pp66, 69, 70, 159,
148, 169(l)
Mark Fiennes p163 (third row, r)
Mark Fiennes/Arcaid p114
Paul Harmer/*Building* p134
Andrew Holmes/Architectural
Association p163(third row, l)

Joel Hopkins p31(b)
Michael Hopkins 33
Pat Hunt p230
Alaistair Hunter pp110, 118
Helmut Jacobi pp21(l), 146
(perspective)
A F Kersting p21(r)
Ken Kirkwood/AFAEP pp13,
38–47, 231
Lance Knobel p163(second row)
Charles MacCullum p163(b)
Eric de Maré pp12, 15, 16, 18–20, 57
James Mortimer pp30, 31(t,m)
Ove Arup & Partners pp60, 68
Alberto Piovano/Arcaid p116
Tim Street Porter pp26, 32
Royal Commission on the Historical

Monuments of England p8
Richard Rogers + Partners p233(b)
Sir Norman Foster and Partners
p233(t)
Timothy Soar pp61, 72–3, 76–7, 130,
135, 138–42, 143(b), 144
Morley von Sternberg pp54–5, 177
Rupert Truman pp11, 24(l), 25(r)
Bill Tuomey p29
Matthew Weinreb pp34–7

Phaidon Press wishes to thank
Andrew Mead for his assistance.
Michael Hopkins and Partners
thanks Clare Endicott for her
pictorial and general assistance
with this book

Michael Hopkins:
a critical biography

Colin Davies

New Parliamentary
Building, Westminster,
London, 1989–.

When Michael Hopkins was a pupil at Sherbourne School he regularly skipped games by taking bicycle rides into the surrounding Dorset countryside to study the local country houses and parish churches. It is tempting to see in this early enthusiasm for old buildings and picturesque landscapes the roots of an undeniable but difficult to define Englishness in his own architecture. Its real significance, however, is not in the buildings that he sketched and photographed but in the extracurricular nature of the activity. Right from the start, architecture represented an escape from the dull conformity of the classroom and the playing field. In Hopkins' mind, it has remained something outside the sort of daily routines to which most people have to submit in order to make their way in the world. It is a love more than a duty, an art more than a profession, a personal enthusiasm more than a job. Had circumstances contrived to deflect Hopkins into some other business or profession, then architecture would certainly have been his hobby; not the architecture of the history books and the tourist trail, but the absorbing practical art of designing and constructing buildings. Hopkins takes his architecture home with him. His marriage partner, Patty, is also his professional partner and, when the couple set up in practice on their own account, they combined home and office without any apparent strain or conflict. The demands of running a large and busy practice may now govern their daily lives, but architecture itself still retains the pleasurable associations of a bike ride in the countryside.

As the son of a builder running a medium-size firm in Bournemouth, it is not surprising that Hopkins was encouraged by his parents to think of architecture as a career. But they did not have to encourage very hard. He remembers that, as a child, he always had some kind of building project in hand, such as redesigning his bedroom or fixing up small boats. He was not, and is still not, good with his hands, but solving constructional problems has always given him great satisfaction. In the years since, this habit of often having a personal building project on the go has become something like a second career, intersecting here and there with the mainstream of his professional life. In

his early student years, he undertook the restoration of a 9 metre lugger, with the intention of sailing it across the channel. Later on, while studying at the Architectural Association in London, he and Patty used the money earned designing a temporary band stand for a jazz festival to buy an old, derelict, timber-framed house in Suffolk. It was the cheapest property on a list of threatened buildings drawn up by the Society for the Protection of Ancient Buildings. Patty, also a student at the AA, took the house as the subject of her measured-drawing assignment, and the couple embarked on a restoration programme that was to take 10 years. They still own and use the house, but it was the urge to build something that really motivated them.

There is an obvious connection between 16th century vernacular, timber-frame architecture and the skeletal, metal and glass buildings that Hopkins designed in the early phase of his career. He maintains that he learned a lot about materials and structures from this first major hands-on experience of building construction. Some of those lessons were later applied to the Hopkins House in Hampstead, London, a personal project that, as it were, crossed over into his professional and public career. The building in Marylebone, London, that Hopkins designed in 1983 to accommodate his burgeoning practice might also be said to straddle the personal and professional worlds. And, in 1987, Michael and Patty Hopkins embarked on another ambitious private project – the restoration of a villa at Lucca in Tuscany. That project continues and its lessons are still being learned.

Education and exploration

No-one would describe Hopkins as an academic type, but when he left school at 17 he got a place on the architecture course at Bournemouth Art School and began preparing external 'testimonies of study' for submission to the Royal Institute of British Architects in London. He left the art school after 18 months because he did not find the course absorbing and began to work for a local architect. Shortly afterwards Frederick Gibberd came to Bournemouth to give a lecture on modern

Michael and Patty Hopkins' 400-year-old house in Suffolk.

architecture and Hopkins wrote to him for a job. The application was successful and for the next two years Hopkins worked for Gibberd in London. The stint with Gibberd was followed by six months working for the Church Commissioners on the restoration of Southwell Minster and then two years working for Sir Basil Spence. Meanwhile, the preparation of testimonies continued, but it had become obvious to Hopkins that full-time education was a better way to achieve his ambitions. He determined to pursue his studies at what was considered the best school in the country, the Architectural Association.

Hoping for admission to the fourth year, he had to settle for a second-year place. More than five years of office experience might have been a practical asset to him, but it did not impress his new teachers who declared his testimonies to be dull and unimaginative. The first two years at the AA were a loosening-up period. As well as methodical exercises in the design of individual buildings, the projects included a village study, tutored by Elizabeth Chesterton, which encouraged a broader view of the cultural and social aspects of architecture. But Hopkins learned as much from his fellow students as from his teachers. The list of his peers is impressive: Birkin Haward, Peter Rich, Mike Gold, Chris Cross, Michael Pearce and Ed Jones – all were later to make names for themselves either as practising architects or as teachers. Hopkins shared a flat with a fifth-year student, Tim Tinker, and through him was introduced to the particular intellectual strain of architectural discourse being promoted at that time by the dominant spirit at the AA, Peter Smithson. Smithson set the intellectual agenda for the whole school. He emphasised the importance of place and context in architecture, but always insisted that projects be building-centred. The AA, he said, was a school of architecture, not a school of sociology. Smithson, however, was far from being the only serious architectural thinker at the AA in the late 1950s. Other members of staff included Bob Maxwell, Alan Colquhoun, Cedric Price and John Winter.

Typically, extracurricular activities also contributed to Hopkins' education, in particular a friendship with the architect Oliver Hill. It had been Landfall, a house in Poole designed by

Oliver Hill: Landfall, Poole, Dorset, 1939.

Hill and owned by friends of the Hopkins family, that had first revealed to Hopkins the exciting spatial and structural possibilities of Modernist architecture. While at the AA he became Hill's protégé and the two collaborated on various small projects. Hill's relaxed approach to architecture – he was as happy designing in a neo-Georgian as in a Modernist style – seemed to harden, rather than soften, Hopkins' personal ideology. John Winter, who was later to develop a ruthlessly Modern style best represented by his own steel and glass house in Highgate, London, was Hopkins' tutor for a typically complex, fourth-year urban-design project. At this point, Hopkins began to develop an expertise in the planning of large-scale, medium-density, mixed developments that he put to good use in the years immediately after qualifying. Efficient, economical planning was the most highly valued skill in these advanced student projects. Social framework, density and movement patterns were more important than construction and materials. A steel or concrete frame was taken for granted, with external walls mostly of glass. Elevations were a direct expression of plan and section, and unquestionably modern in appearance. If architectural precedents were evoked, they were probably Scandinavian buildings by Alvar Aalto or Ralph Erskine, or alternatively the reductive Corbusian slab blocks of the London County Council's Alton Estate housing scheme in Roehampton. The word style was never uttered.

After leaving college in 1963, Hopkins got a job with Leonard Manasseh, working on the design of new halls of residence at Leicester University. There he saw the recently completed Engineering Building by James Stirling and James Gowan – a powerful neo-Constructivist composition in red tile-clad concrete and patent glazing. This building could hardly fail to make an impression on Hopkins, as it did on just about every other British architect at the time. He greatly admired it, though it cannot be said to have had any great influence on his own architecture. What he remembers most vividly is the surprisingly hostile reaction of the university bursar to a building that the architectural profession was calling a masterpiece. The Manasseh halls of residence building was a more conventional Modernist exercise in concrete and brick. For Hopkins its value was as an introduction to traditional contractual procedures – slow, complicated and inefficient. He also worked on a medium-density housing scheme in Basildon – 80 people per acre with a 'Radburn' plan that segregated vehicles and pedestrians.

His next job was with Tom Hancock, working on plans for the expansion of Peterborough as part of the government's new-town strategy. Here he applied the planning skills he had gained at the AA to real projects at a truly urban scale. For two years he worked on huge masterplans for housing up to 100,000 people. The projects were overtaken by the advent of development corporations and never got off the drawing board, but Hopkins had learned some important professional lessons from Hancock – how to interpret a brief imaginatively and how to sell an idea to a client.

By this time, Patty was starting to make her architectural contribution to the partnership. In 1967, her final AA project was for a health centre, using the principles of the Californian School Construction System, which was not so much a building system in the conventional sense as a bulk-buying policy for building components. Here was a vision of building no longer tied to the old, site-based craft traditions but taking advantage of large-scale factory production. The prime example of this particular approach, and one that had a profound influence on Michael and Patty Hopkins, was the house that Charles and Ray Eames constructed for themselves in Santa Monica, USA, in 1949. This bolt-together assemblage of off-the-peg, steel and glass components seemed to point a new way forward for building technology and to free architecture from the last vestiges of academic stuffiness. Patty's health centre design was well received by the project jury, which included the young Norman Foster.

By this time Hopkins' father had become a director of the development wing of a national contracting firm. It was an obvious source of possible work and, in 1968, it at last produced a commission – to plan an industrial estate at Goole in Yorkshire. To do the job, Hopkins needed an experienced partner with an established office. Team 4 – the partnership between Norman and Wendy Foster, and Richard and Su Rogers, had recently broken up. Foster was looking for work and Hopkins had a job in his pocket. Their partnership lasted for the next eight years.

The Goole job came to nothing, but Foster and Hopkins shared an enthusiasm for that vision of a new kind of architecture represented by the Californian houses of Rafael Soriano, Craig Ellwood and, of course, Charles and Ray Eames. Foster's amenity building in the London docks for the Fred Olsen shipping line had already impressed the critics by the simplicity of its plan and its minimal structure, clad entirely in mirror glass. When Philip Dowson, a founder member of Arup Associates, recommended Foster Associates to IBM for the design of a temporary office building at Cosham in Hampshire, Hopkins got his first opportunity to work in the new idiom.

On the face of it the brief was unpromising. IBM simply wanted a plan for a group of temporary buildings to accommodate 750 office workers while their new Portsmouth headquarters was built. But put in more abstract terms, a cheap, fast, short-life, flexible building was required. Foster and Hopkins dutifully presented a number of proposals, including evaluations of various off-the-peg systems, but their preferred

Above, Foster Associates:
IBM Cosham, Hampshire,
1971.
Right, Charles and Ray
Eames: the Eames House,
Santa Monica, 1949.

solution was a purpose-designed, single-storey, deep-planned, rectangular slab. This design was costed and programmed and the client was duly persuaded.

Almost everything in the Cosham building was inspired by American practice. Like the Eames House and the Californian School Construction System, it was constructed from factory-made metal components: profiled-metal roof decking on lightweight, lattice-steel beams and slender steel columns. Like a New York office block, it was 'space planned' within a deep, air-conditioned envelope with a sealed, external skin. The skin was all glass – storey-height sheets, with no transoms, fascias or spandrel panels, held in neoprene gaskets of the type common in the USA but relatively new to Britain. Air conditioning was provided not by a conventional central system, but by local roof-mounted modules of American design. Even the organisation of its construction was American. There was no main contractor, and specialist subcontractors and suppliers were co-ordinated on site by the architects. Above all, the building was utterly simple and practical. There were very few details and each element was designed to be built quickly and cheaply so that the money could be spent where it counted – on high-quality, durable materials: steel and glass replacing the timber and plywood of the available temporary building systems.

Working on Cosham, Hopkins found himself back in the world of real building projects, like the cross-Channel lugger and the house in Suffolk. The tighter the constraints of time and cost, the more fun it was finding simple, elegant solutions. These solutions lay not in the traditional craft-based building industry, but in the catalogues of American component manufacturers and their infant British counterparts. The shape of the new architecture was now clear in Hopkins' mind. Its forms were simple. The traditional Modernist conception of a close fit between function and plan was questioned. IBM assumed they would need three buildings: one for the offices, one for the computers and one for the staff amenities. But Cosham demonstrated that all could be accommodated in a single envelope, with no loss of quality and with the benefit of

flexibility. The building could be out of the ground before the brief was settled, and when the requirements changed, which they inevitably would, a new plan arrangement could be accommodated with considerable ease.

Most importantly, however, the buildings of the new architecture could be made using the materials and techniques of industrial production, just like cars, caravans, refrigerators, typewriters or aeroplanes. The environment they created would be cleaner, brighter, more open to change and more optimistic about the future. All this had been said before, of course, as Hopkins himself pointed out in a lecture to the Royal Society of Arts in London, in 1991: 'Le Corbusier, in the 1920s, exhorted architects and builders to look around them at what was being developed in related fields: ship engineering, aeronautical engineering, automobile engineering ... In America, Buckminster Fuller used the surplus aircraft production capability after the war by developing a high performance, lightweight house that could be produced at the rate of 200 a day from the Beech Aircraft Corporation Factory. This was the Wichita House. It never got beyond the prototype stage but, nevertheless, the dream persisted to encourage the next generation.' Foster and Hopkins saw themselves as the heirs of Buckminster Fuller, but they were not content with prototypes: they wanted to do it for real.

The next major project on which Hopkins worked in the Foster office was the now famous office building for Willis Faber & Dumas in Ipswich. With this job the stakes were suddenly raised. The new architecture had to prove that it could work not just for a cheap, temporary building on an open site, but also for a permanent, prestige headquarters in a town centre. The building is remarkable for its planning innovations, especially the dramatic cascade of escalators in the top-lit central atrium and the serpentine perimeter wall. And yet in its way it is every bit as simple and abstract as Cosham. Its office floors are flexible, serviced zones, waiting to be space-planned, and its external wall is the ultimate minimalist enclosure: a hanging curtain of entirely frameless, butt-jointed glass. At the time it was hailed as a contextual building because the glass

Buckminster Fuller: Wichita House prototype, 1946.

wall not only conformed to the irregular street pattern but literally reflected the surrounding buildings. Looking back at it now, Hopkins acknowledges that this was a sort of sleight of hand, no more than a lucky accident. There are aspects of Willis Faber Dumas that he now finds unsatisfactory. The entrance to the building, for example, looks like an afterthought, an unwelcome blemish in the perfection of the glass skin. Simplicity of detail had become such an obsession that the architecture would not even allow the special case of a proper front door. Willis Faber Dumas was, and still is, a great building, but in later years Hopkins was to tackle the question of urban context in a very different way.

Breaking new ground

By 1976 Hopkins knew exactly what he wanted to do architecturally and his client contacts were sufficiently well established for him to set up his own small practice. He and Patty needed a London base that would match their professional and architectural aspirations. They decided to design themselves a house, which would be the family home for themselves and their three children as well as being an architectural manifesto and a demonstration piece for potential clients. And it would be a joy to build – the most satisfying private project yet. The Eames House was the inspiration, but the site, among the big old houses of conservative Hampstead, was a long way from the laid back, sunny suburbia of Pacific Palisades. Nevertheless, there was no compromise. The house makes no conventional concessions to its mature context. It is a simple, abstract assemblage of factory-made, steel and glass components.

   The house has become an icon. It has entered the artistic canon of modern architecture and is identified not by its address but by the name of its owners. Like the Farnsworth House, the Robie House and the Eames House, it is known simply as the Hopkins House. The Eames House may have been its inspiration, but the resemblance is conceptual rather than architectural. Laid-back it is not. Rather it is obsessively rigorous and controlled. The components from which it is assembled –

Foster Associates:
Willis Faber Dumas,
Ipswich, 1975.

profiled metal sheeting (for both walls and floor), steel lattice trusses and very large sheets of glass – have an as-found, industrial quality, but they are put together with a care and precision that is more Germanic than American, more Mies van der Rohe than Charles Eames. The aim of this particular architectural game is to make a building with the fewest possible components joined together in the fewest possible ways. Half a dozen constructional details are sufficient to describe the whole structure and each one is completely resolved. As Hopkins himself has said: 'The corner-eaves junction is always for us an amazing achievement, because all the systems in the house come together in that one point, and they fit.' The original design was even simpler, with glass walls all round. The profiled-steel flanks were introduced later to satisfy fire regulations.

As with Willis Faber Dumas, this minimalist approach tends to undermine traditional architectural expectations. There are few concessions to domestic privacy in the division of the internal space, despite the fact that the building was originally used as an office as well as a house. Front and back facades are made entirely of storey-height glass panes, and that includes the front door. A perforated metal bridge marks the entrance, but there is no sheltering porch. Although its low thermal capacity and large areas of glazing might not seem ideal from the point of view of environmental comfort, the compact form of the building and its sheltered, south-facing prospect make it comfortable and economical to run. Michael and Patty Hopkins have proved that it works. They still enjoy living in the house and have adapted it flexibly over the years to the shifting requirements of office and home.

The house has worked also as a public relations vehicle. The critical acclaim it received established the Hopkins name and a few commercial and industrial clients were impressed enough to offer him commissions. The buildings he designed between 1977 and 1984 all display the basic concerns that are demonstrated in the house. At the time a number of British architects were developing a similar approach. It came to be known, much to the annoyance of its practitioners, including

Hopkins House,
Hampstead,
London, 1976.

Hopkins, as 'British High-Tech'. The annoyance perhaps arose because, though the similarities were undeniable and three of the main protagonists (Hopkins, Foster and Rogers) had worked together and clearly influenced one another's thinking, there were also important differences. For example, Rogers' desire to give architectural expression to mechanical services by putting the pipes and ducts on the outside of the building, of which the best example is the Pompidou Centre in Paris, completed in 1977, was certainly not shared by either Hopkins or Foster.

Three projects from this period – Greene King, Patera and Schlumberger – serve to illustrate the main characteristics of the developing Hopkins style. None of them was required to respond in any positive way to an existing built context. The Greene King Draught Beer Cellars in Bury St Edmunds and the Schlumberger Cambridge Research Centre occupy open greenfield sites, and Patera is a standard design developed without any specific location in mind. In this respect, and in many others, these are more like products than buildings, more like industrial design than architecture. They even appear to be portable, like large pieces of mechanical equipment. Le Corbusier's 'machines for living in' looked nothing like machines, unless you count the superstructures of ocean liners. Hopkins' early buildings really do have a machine-like quality. The Greene King building is raised off the ground for good practical reasons – to keep it above the flood level and to simplify the design of the loading bays – but this creates the illusion that it has been delivered to site in one piece, perhaps airlifted in by helicopter. The office wings of Schlumberger also sit lightly on their grassy banks, and of course the big fabric structure stretched between them looks like nothing so much as a circus tent, likely to be packed up and carted away tomorrow.

Another common characteristic of these early buildings is their repetitive, linear, indeterminate configuration. All are single-storey designs with uni-directional structures. They could be lengthened indefinitely without destroying any essential aspect of their architecture. One might describe them as 'extruded' were it not for the fact that each bay is clearly expressed. Even the plain, horizontally profiled metal flank walls of Greene King are divided vertically into panels. This injects a proportional discipline but more importantly it implies that they might one day be dismantled and re-erected elsewhere – which may well happen if the planned sideways extension is ever built.

The architecture thus becomes a direct expression of the prefabricated and potentially demountable nature of the construction. This 'kit-of-parts' approach is, at one level, a practical strategy, but it is also an aesthetic preference. Traditional materials like brick and concrete might have done the job just as well, and possibly more cheaply, but they would not have conveyed the same message of faith in the benefits of industrial technology.

But Hopkins was interested in more than just the semblance of industrial production. It was not enough that his buildings should look mass produced – he wanted to design a real mass-produced building. Architects who try to imitate the methods of manufacturing industry face a special problem. It takes many years of research and development to design a new car. This costs a great deal of money and demands the production and marketing of thousands of more or less identical products in order to recoup the investment. Buildings are usually one-offs designed for specific sites. Protracted development programmes are therefore economically out of the question. There are two possible solutions to this problem. The first is to develop factory-made building components that can be used on a large number of different buildings. The second is to mass produce complete buildings.

In 1983 Hopkins got the chance to try out this latter solution when Nigel Dale, the grandson of the chairman of a steel-fabrication firm and an ex-architect, commissioned him to design a small, high-quality, standard industrial building suitable for almost any site. For Hopkins this was a dream job, a chance to do for real the sort of project that he might have invented in his spare time.

The Patera project was an attempt to bring to building some of the engineering refinement of car production. It is Hopkins' version of Buckminster Fuller's Wichita House. Buildings like

Greene King Draught
Beer Cellars, Bury St
Edmunds, Suffolk, 1981.

Cosham, the Hopkins House or Greene King are assemblages of industrial components designed by others. There might have been some opportunity to adapt these components in small ways for particular applications, but still many of the major design decisions were outside the control of the architect. With Patera, Hopkins had, for the first time, total control in the factory as well as on site. There would not be, of course, thousands of standard buildings produced, but Hopkins hoped there might be a few dozen, which would justify a greater investment in research and development. Like a car, the detailed design of the Patera building was influenced as much by the demands of the manufacturing and assembly processes as by the demands of the market.

In its basic form the building has the same characteristics as Greene King and Schlumberger – a simple, linear, repetitive structure – but the research and development process, which included the building and testing of a complete full-size prototype, achieved a far greater degree of refinement. Similar small industrial or office buildings were appearing in their hundreds on industrial estates and 'science parks' all over the country, but none could compare with the sleek, glossy, almost toy-like quality of the Patera buildings. Just as Le Corbusier had compared the design of his purist villas with that of his favourite Voisin automobile, Hopkins could park his Porsche in front of a

Patera Building System
prototype unit, Stoke on
Trent, 1982.

Patera building and invite a similar comparison. And at least one feature of the building was directly inspired by the design of cars: the same form of construction – insulated metal panels with joints sealed by neoprene gaskets – was used for both the walls and the roof.

In reality, of course, a small industrial building is not required to fulfil the same performance criteria as a sports car. Patera is a sophisticated product only when compared with traditional buildings and Hopkins' claims for it are relatively modest. He sees the fabrication process as roughly comparable to secondary car-production lines in the years immediately after the First World War. In present-day terms, perhaps the closest parallel is with a 'handmade' English sports car like the Morgan rather than with the products of Dagenham or Luton. This is an apt parallel in another sense too. Whereas Buckminster Fuller urged architects to see buildings as short-life products, part of what he called the 'ephemeralisation' of everyday objects, Hopkins is loath to see his buildings put on the scrapheap. In 1992 he was restoring one of the original Patera buildings for use as an extension to his own Marylebone office (itself a version of the Patera concept) in the same way that an enthusiast might restore a vintage or classic car. It seems that these mass-produced buildings still have some of the power of traditional buildings to gather sentimental associations and become permanent fixtures of life.

Patera and Schlumberger share another feature that is typical of High-Tech buildings of the early 1980s: their steel structures are exposed on the outside of the building. The office and laboratory wings of Schlumberger have external steel trusses that are a development of, or rather a simplifications of, the lattice portal frames of Patera. There are functional justifications for the use of this device, as indeed there are for all aspects of Hopkins' architecture. Putting the structure on the outside creates clean, uninterrupted, internal wall and ceiling surfaces. It also means that the volume enclosed by the external envelope is reduced without decreasing the headroom. There is less air to heat, and the building is therefore cheaper to run. Similarly the dramatic external tension structures that support the tents at Schlumberger are able to make good structural use of an infinite amount of space without getting in the way of the drilling rigs inside. But there are just as many good practical reasons for not using external structures. The steelwork is exposed to the weather and harder to maintain, and on flat roofs the waterproof membrane has to be punctured by structural connections, increasing the risk of leaks. As Hopkins readily admits, the preference for external structures is as much aesthetic as practical. In his eyes modern buildings look best when under construction, before the powerful formal statement of the structural frame disappears behind the external cladding. Putting the frame on the outside is a way of preserving this objective, Cartesian quality in the completed building.

When he gives lectures on his work, Hopkins juxtaposes images of Crystal Palace and Schlumberger Cambridge Research Centre. He shares an enthusiasm for the steel and glass exhibition halls and railway stations of the 19th century with the other exponents of the British High-Tech style. But whereas the exposed steel-framed buildings of, for example, Nicholas Grimshaw, tend to make more of the masts and tension cables than can be strictly justified on functional grounds, Hopkins' approach is more restrained. Only the tents of Schlumberger attain anything like the same expressiveness, and here there is ample functional justification. Hopkins is, at heart, a practical problem solver. The covert symbolism of High-Tech was always a secondary issue and in his later buildings he abandoned it completely.

Before leaving this first group of buildings from the early 1980s it is worth pointing out one more device that Hopkins makes use of in later buildings: the fully enclosed, but quasi-external space. The traditional architecture of northern Europe typically conceives of only two categories of space: inside and outside. In-between spaces such as verandas, arcades, loggias and belvederes are not, for obvious reasons, as important as they are in the architectures of warmer climates. In the Schlumberger building Hopkins discovered that for certain uses – the test station and the staff restaurant – ambient temperatures lower than the statutory 21°C were perfectly

Top, Joseph Paxton:
Crystal Palace, Hyde Park,
London, 1851.
Bottom, Schlumberger
Cambridge Research
Centre, Cambridge, 1985.

acceptable, even preferable. The right environmental conditions could therefore be created without enclosing the space in a fully insulated envelope. This had a liberating effect on the form of the building, allowing the replacement of solid walls and roof by a single membrane of Teflon-coated glass fibre. It is no accident that this material, which was new to Britain at that time, had commonly been used in the USA to enclose another kind of in-between space – the shopping mall. It is no accident either that Hopkins had previously worked on the refurbishment of a still unbuilt project for the 1960s' shopping precinct in Basildon, which involved enclosing the town square with a fabric roof and glass end walls. Hopkins' name is now firmly associated with the development of the architectural potential of fabric structures in Britain. The real significance of this aspect of his architecture, however, is not in the flamboyant forms of the tents themselves but in the concept of an in-between space suitable for the British climate. It is primarily an environmental, rather than a purely architectural device. In his later buildings it was developed in a variety of ways, not all of them involving fabric structures.

A reconciliation with history

In the early 1980s Hopkins' architectural philosophy was dominated by the idea of the building as an industrial product. It was made in a factory, it looked like a machine and it was demountable. Its design, therefore, was not influenced by the unique characteristics of any particular site. This was fine as long as the commissions were for simple industrial buildings in non-urban locations. But in 1984 the practice was invited to submit proposals for the rebuilding of the Mound Stand at Lord's Cricket Ground. Suddenly Hopkins was forced to tackle a site with a context – not just the urban context of St John's Wood in London, but also the historical context of a 200-year-old national institution. Continuity, tradition and history could no longer be left out of the architectural equation. After years of looking forward optimistically to the future, he was obliged to turn and engage with the past – not the past of the architectural history books, but the past that lay all around, in the existing buildings on the site, in the surrounding city streets, in the memories of the men that ran the Marylebone Cricket Club, and in the tradition-soaked game of cricket itself.

This was a special problem for Hopkins. After the collapse of what has come to be known as the Modernist consensus in the late 1960s, architects rediscovered the virtues of the traditional city. The Modernist attempts to sweep away the past and replan cities from scratch in a rational, scientific way had been discredited in the public mind. All the talk was of 'contextualism', of preserving the best of the past and of rebuilding the city in a gradual way by sensitive, well-mannered interventions. 'Well-mannered' commonly meant imitating the architecture of neighbouring buildings. And this meant imitating the architecture of the past. In architects' offices all over the western world, the history books were taken down and dusted off, and once again traditional Classical details were beginning to appear in new buildings, though often they never penetrated further than the facades. Post-Modernism became the new orthodoxy.

All this was anathema to Hopkins, who remained a Modernist at heart. He believed in the benefits of technology and of inventive design and he had little knowledge or appreciation of architectural history. But at Lord's, of all places,

Mound Stand,
Lord's Cricket Ground,
London, 1987.

context and tradition seemed inescapable. It is characteristic of the way in which Hopkins' architecture has developed that he chose not to dodge this issue but to tackle it head on. Here was a new problem to be solved and solve it he did. He might reasonably have ignored the context and built a purely functional grandstand, possibly as the first phase of a complete rebuilding programme that would eventually convert Lord's into a modern stadium. Instead he looked at the physical and historical context of the site and tried to find a way of responding to it without resorting to the meaningless imitation of historical forms that he so despised in the architecture of his Post-Modern contemporaries.

The starting point was an existing structure – the brick arcade that formed part of the base of the old Mound Stand. Hopkins decided to preserve this arcade, and even extend it, imitating precisely the form of the original. On the face of it this was precisely what he had set out not to do. But it could be justified philosophically on the grounds that it was simply the completion of a job that Frank Verity had started 100 years before but had been unable to finish because he ran out of money. There was a good practical reason for preserving the arcade. It meant that building work could proceed in two winter phases, allowing the refurbished lower tier of seating to be used during the intervening summer. Nevertheless, the decision represents a turning point in the development of Hopkins' architectural philosophy. The preservation of an existing structure, the imitation of an old building and the use of a traditional, low-tech material – all these were new departures. There is no precedent for them in Hopkins' previous buildings.

Despite these innovations, the design of this part of the Mound Stand remains typical of Hopkins' work in one very important respect. At this point in the story it is necessary to pause and examine what might be described as the cornerstone of his philosophy: truth to materials. The honest expression of structure and construction has been an important theme in the development of modern architecture since the mid-19th century. It was then that Gothic architecture was rediscovered,

not just as a style but as what we now call engineering. To such theorists as A W N Pugin and Viollet le Duc, the Gothic cathedral seemed to represent the ultimate development of the structural potential of stone. Architectural form seemed to arise naturally from the characteristics of the material. This 'honest' Christian architecture was contrasted with the 'decadent' pagan architecture of the Renaissance, which was more concerned with the ornamentation of buildings using ancient Classical forms than with the direct expression of structure. Ever since Pugin, architects have been divided broadly into two camps: Gothic and Renaissance. According to this crude dichotomy High-Tech can be seen as Gothic, and Post-Modernism as Renaissance.

We have seen how Hopkins' early buildings were attempts to make a new architecture out of the realities of industrial production, and how the steel-frame structures are always clearly visible, sometimes on the outside of the buildings. We must now recognise, however, that these are really different aspects of a single guiding principle: that the fabric of a building (to paraphrase Pugin) should consist only of what is essential to its construction. In other words, there should be no fake finishes, no facades divorced from plan and function, no deliberate concealment. The structural materials should be clearly visible but, more than that, the forms of the architecture should derive directly from the nature of those materials and of the techniques used to fashion them. Though the materials and techniques might differ, this principle nevertheless holds true for all Hopkins' buildings. It is his architectural guiding light and his guarantee of authenticity.

To return to Lord's, most architects, had they chosen to extend Verity's arcade, would have been content to put up a steel or concrete frame and attach brickwork to it in imitation of the original but with completely different structural characteristics. But if Hopkins was going to use this, to him, unfamiliar material, he was going to use it properly. His arches would be real arches and they would really bear load. He found a way to be contextual without sacrificing honesty. Paradoxically, the principle of truth to materials that is such an

Mound Stand, Lord's
Cricket Ground, London,
1987.

important aspect of High-Tech building, led him away from industrial production, back to a traditional site-based craft.

But this was no Pauline conversion. It was simply a pragmatic response to the problems of phasing and context. The rest of the new stand is a modern, metal and glass structure, innovative and structurally daring. We must remember that this is Hopkins' first major multi-storey building. To balance the whole superstructure on a single row of steel masts is daring indeed and has nothing to do with traditional crafts. Here is a rational solution to a practical problem, using to the full the structural potential of steel in the form of massive plate girders. And here again we have another version of the in-between space idea. Much of the seating is in the open air, sheltered only from the rain, but in a sense the enclosed parts of the building – the hospitality boxes, bars and restaurants – are also in-between spaces. Since they are used only in summer, they are unheated and uninsulated, often with only a thin sheet of steel or glass to separate inside from the outside.

To finish the whole building off with a festive fabric canopy was an almost inevitable gesture, given the precedents of Schlumberger and Basildon. Here it is irresistibly appropriate, evoking as it does associations of marquees on village greens. And the associations are not accidental. Hopkins' whole idea was to maintain the picturesque character of Lord's, not as a single unified stadium but as a disparate collection of relatively small buildings, retaining something of cricket's rural roots. He was responding to the historical and sentimental context as well as to the physical surroundings. In this single building, he opened up his architecture to encompass worlds not thought of in his days of High-Tech orthodoxy.

The Mound Stand was completed in 1987 and was well received in cricketing and architectural circles. Sited beside the most televised strip of turf in England, and with all the sweet overtones of leather, willow and national pride, it could hardly have been a better advertisement for Hopkins' architecture. It received a royal seal of approval from the Prince of Wales, the leader of anti-Modernist opinion, and it was seized upon by professional critics as a rare example of a truly popular modern

building. Hopkins joined the select group of practising architects whose names are known outside the profession. His practice was, by this time, well established. The office had outgrown the Hampstead house, first overflowing into a neighbouring property and then moving into a larger version of a Patera building on the outer fringe of Marylebone. The internal culture of the practice was also maturing. Hopkins' most talented young assistants, John Pringle, Ian Sharratt and Bill Taylor, were made partners and began to make their contribution to the rapidly developing architectural language of the practice.

The new elements in the architecture came about partly because of the influence of these partners but Hopkins retained, and still retains, the design initiative on every project. He prides himself on his ability to produce outline schemes very quickly. These are developed by other designers in the office and put before Hopkins, who then suggests the direction of further development. Since constructional details are as important in his architecture as plans and sections, this process continues through every stage from first sketches to working drawings.

Hopkins' growing confidence in his abilities allowed him to experiment with a much wider variety of forms and techniques. If the High-Tech phase of his career was characterised by

Fleet Velmead Infants
School, Hampshire, 1986.

progressive simplification and refinement, this new phase was more relaxed, more outward looking and above all more responsive to context. Every new job was an opportunity to develop and enrich the language. 1988 saw the completion of three more buildings, all on rural sites but otherwise bearing no obvious resemblance to one another.

In the Fleet Velmead Infants School in Hampshire, commissioned by the progressive local authority architect Colin Stansfield Smith, the techniques developed in the early industrial buildings were applied to the more complex brief and more sensitive environmental requirements of a primary school. The building is single storey, with the usual plain rectangular plan form and a simple, repetitive, linear structure of tubular steel. The roof is profiled metal, with a glazed clerestory above a central circulation spine, and the walls are mostly glass. Internally the different functions are accommodated in 'buildings-within-a-building' – a device first used to serve the very different functional needs of the Greene King brewery. The typical modern primary school has a complex, articulated plan – a collection of linked pavilions of different sizes to enclose the wide variety of spaces from the head teacher's office to the main assembly hall. Fleet Velmead Infants School demonstrates that these functions can all be accommodated satisfactorily in a single, economical envelope. It is an idea that goes all the way back to IBM at Cosham.

The client for the Solid State Logic building at Begbroke, near Oxford, was of a more familiar type: a company manufacturing recording equipment that wanted a building combining the functions of office and factory sited in the garden of its country house headquarters. A few years earlier this commission would almost certainly have resulted in a version of the Patera building – a High-Tech building for a High-Tech client.

The building that was constructed has some of the expected features – a flexible floor plan and walls of metal and glass – but it differs from the Patera model in three important ways. First it has two storeys. This would not be remarkable except that, for the first time, it allowed Hopkins to introduce a double-height volume in the form of a central top-lit atrium. This has

dramatically different spatial consequences. In the earlier single-storey buildings, the internal space has an abstract, diagrammatic quality. It is simply a flexible, serviced zone, ready to be divided up in various ways to suit various functions. The configuration is always subject to change. But in the Solid State Logic building the usable floor areas are all related to the permanently defined space of the atrium. The whole interior therefore has a unified, centred quality not hitherto seen in Hopkins' architecture.

This centredness is reflected in the second important difference between this building and the Patera precedent: the plan is square, instead of rectangular. Instead of an infinitely extendible row of steel frames, the building has a two-way structure on a square grid of columns. Its form is finite and would be difficult to extend because the first floor overhangs the ground floor on all four sides. A two-directional floor with cantilevers is a structural form more suited to concrete than steel.

And this is the third new feature: the architectural use of in-situ concrete. In Hopkins' previous buildings this wet, messy, site-crafted material had been confined to foundations and ground-floor slabs. For the visible parts of the building he had always preferred clean, dry materials like metal and glass.

Solid State Logic
Research and
Development Building,
Begbroke, Oxford, 1988.

Characteristically, when obliged to use concrete, he decided to expose it to view and to give honest expression to its moulded nature. There is, therefore, no suspended ceiling to conceal the soffit of the first-floor slab, which has shallow, circular coffers to accommodate the light fittings. This kind of heavy, monolithic, permanent structure is one more new element in the developing Hopkins language.

The little cutlery factory in Hathersage, Derbyshire is, perhaps, the most interesting of the trio of buildings completed in 1988. Here the plan is not just centred, it is circular. The circular plan form was exploited deliberately in many later projects but this first occurrence came about almost by accident. The rural site is a sensitive one from a planning point of view. By proposing to reuse the base of an old gasholder, Hopkins persuaded the local planners that the new building was simply the replacement of an old one. As with the Mound Stand, the remains of an existing structure were the starting point for the design. But Hopkins was prepared to go even further than at Lord's to acknowledge the historical and physical context of the site. Two buildings had survived from the original Victorian gasworks. They were of local stone, with steel roof structures, in what J M Richards called the 'functional tradition' of the 19th century; their simplicity and honesty appealed to Hopkins and he decided to build a late 20th-century version of them, with real stone walls bearing the load of the great 'bicycle wheel' roof structure. The client, David Mellor, had a personal preference for lead as a building material. In his new, accommodating mood, Hopkins used this as an opportunity to explore yet another new avenue. The lead roof of Hathersage may look traditional, but it is an assemblage of prefabricated panels, not of metal but of plywood. Taking a traditional material and fabricating it in a modern way became a recurring theme in Hopkins' work from then on.

At Hathersage, all vestiges of the High-Tech style have finally disappeared. Nevertheless, this little factory is every bit as true to the technology of its construction as a Patera building. As Hopkins himself put it: 'If everything that you build as you go along is what you finish seeing, then you are going to get some arresting architecture. You see the wall, you see the steel structure, you see the underside of the plywood panels and they become the finish of the building, the interior of the building. All there is on the floor is the paint which goes straight over the concrete slab. If you can keep the finishes of your architecture near to its original surfaces, the chances are that you may achieve some quality in your building.'

Responding to context became an essential part of the Hopkins design process. At Hathersage, he deliberately emphasised quite minor features of the site and surroundings in order to inform his design. But in the next major project the context was impossible to ignore. In 1986, the *Financial Times* joined the exodus of newspapers from Fleet Street to London Docklands. Its owners were faced with the problem of what to do with their old editorial offices and printworks, which occupied a whole city block near St Paul's Cathedral in the heart of the City of London. They decided to redevelop the site and invited six well-known architects, Hopkins among them, to prepare outline proposals. Hopkins won the competition with a design for a new office block but, before the scheme could be developed further, the client decided to sell the site to the Japanese development company, Obayashi. It was perhaps a wise move, because almost immediately the existing building, Bracken House, was deemed to be of special architectural importance and it was listed.This effectively ruled out a complete redevelopment. Some kind of adaptation of the old building, preserving its main architectural features, was the only possibility, and Obayashi duly commissioned Hopkins to prepare a new scheme along these lines.

Hopkins was called upon not just to acknowledge a sensitive urban context but to incorporate an architectural monument, albeit a relatively young one, in his design. Bracken House was designed in the 1950s by Sir Albert Richardson in a vaguely Classical style. Two office wings, built of brick and sandstone with a copper-clad attic storey, flanked a curious octagonal printworks. It was a fine, but flawed, building. The wings were satisfyingly solid and well proportioned, but the printworks was an ugly hybrid structure, neither monumental nor functional.

David Mellor Cutlery Factory, Hathersage, Derbyshire, 1989.

A basic strategy was soon devised: to keep the wings and demolish the printworks, replacing it with a new office building.

The way Hopkins set about realising this strategy is pertinent to the development of his architectural repertoire. For the first time we see him making reference to the established canon of architectural history. Richardson's design, he discovered, was inspired by the form of the 1679 Palazzo Carignano in Turin by Guarino Guarini, which has rectangular wings flanking an oval centre section. In Richardson's Bracken House the oval, for reasons of economy and practicality, had shrunk and become an octagon. Hopkins decided that, just as he had belatedly realised Verity's ambitions at Lord's, he would be true to Richardson's original intentions and reinstate the oval. That Hopkins used an historical precedent outside the Modern tradition at all is remarkable enough; that he chose a building of the 17th-century Italian Baroque is extraordinary. But by this stage he was increasingly on the look out for new opportunities to develop and expand his repertoire. The discovery of Richardson's original inspiration was the starting point he needed. Most modern architects would probably have tackled this problem by simply contrasting the old and new parts of the building. By recovering the spirit of the original design, Hopkins produced not just a new extension but a reinterpretation of the existing building.

The Palazzo Carignano is not the only historical precedent. Students of the history of English architecture will recognise in the metal-and-glass cladding of the new building the influence of Peter Ellis' 1864 Oriel Chambers in Liverpool – a proto-Modernist office block with Gothic overtones. Certainly there is no precedent in Hopkins' own work for this wall of faceted glass held in a delicate, tubular, bronze framework. This is not an arbitrary historical reference, however, but a development of the metal-framed bay windows in the ground floor of Richardson's office wings. The idea comes not from the history book but from the immediate context.

The new facades use the same materials as the existing building: bronze, glass and stone. But this is more than just a superficial 'blending in' to please the planners and English

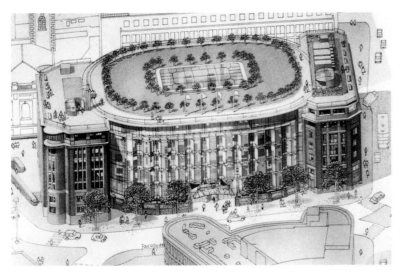

Above, Bracken House,
London, 1992.
Right, Peter Ellis:
Oriel Chambers,
Liverpool, 1864.

Heritage. As in every Hopkins building, the materials are used according to their nature. The solid stone piers support the great splayed brackets, which support the slender bronze columns, that restrain the perimeter of the office floors. It is all real structure. That is what distinguishes it from the 'contextual', but fake, facades of its post-Modern counterparts. Writing about Bracken House in the *Architects' Journal*, Hopkins' AA tutor, John Winter, described this search for new, inventive ways to put buildings together as 'one of the most creative developments on the British architectural scene'.

Hopkins could now speak a variety of architectural languages. Overt historical and contextual references were not appropriate for every project. Two more urban buildings completed at about the same time as Bracken House show him reverting to a more abstract, Modernist discipline. The David Mellor Offices and Showroom at Shad Thames in London is a finely crafted display case, which resembles the surrounding Victorian warehouses only in its austerity and simplicity. Here we are back with the obsessive minimalism of the Hampstead house, except that the structural frame is concrete, not steel, with a consequently greater solidity and ruggedness.

The much larger buildings at New Square, Bedfont Lakes for IBM should not, perhaps, be described as urban, sited as they are on reclaimed land close to Heathrow Airport. Nevertheless an urban precedent is evoked in the masterplan, which is based on Grosvenor Square – not as it exists today but as it was first built in open fields on the edge of the city. The buildings themselves are severely abstract, with ultra-refined exposed steel frames that call to mind Mies van der Rohe's Illinois Institute of Technology. They are Miesian in another sense too – in the Classical formality and symmetry of both site plan and individual buildings. Until now, with the possible exception of Solid State Logic, axial symmetry had only been an incidental quality in Hopkins' buildings. Patera, Schlumberger, Greene King – all are symmetrical in the strictly geometric sense, but the symmetry arises from their structural rationale rather than from any deliberate formality or frontality. But at Bedfont Lakes, the largest of the three Hopkins buildings extends across the whole width of the square like a neo-Classical palace or museum, and most of all like Mies' Crown Hall at IIT, which Hopkins visited and admired while developing the design. The building and its setting are combined in a single, formal, almost monumental composition.

This new formality can also be seen in the extension to the Schlumberger Cambridge Research Centre, completed in 1992. Here the incidental symmetry of the original building is, as it were, converted into formal symmetry by the placing of two square pavilions, each based on the Solid State Logic building, on either side of the axis. In the original building the entrance is simply a series of doors in the flat glass end wall with no formal emphasis. But the extension is provided with a proper double-height entrance hall between the pavilions, with a revolving door, reception desk and spiral staircase all on axis. At one level Hopkins' symmetry is simply an organising device to make plan and structure coherent and legible, but in the later buildings and projects it also becomes a formal and spatial statement, a re-emergence of the strong Classical undercurrent in Miesian Modernism. All the later urban projects have either completely symmetrical plans, or important symmetrical elements.

Success and sensibility

By 1990, Hopkins' professional career had reached the point of lift-off. Every new building and project was featured in the architectural and lay press. He was lecturing to packed audiences, not just in architecture schools but on more public platforms such as the RIBA and the Royal Society of Arts. His was a name to be dropped in any informed company. Colour supplements and women's magazines carried interviews with the man who represented the human face of Modernism. There were frequent television appearances. He had become an establishment figure. As a member of the Royal Fine Arts Commission he was called upon to give judgements upon the nation's most important building projects – except, that is, for his own. His was a national, not yet an international, reputation but his very Britishness may have given him a competitive edge in the home market. While the other big names of British architecture sought commissions abroad to maintain the momentum of their careers, Hopkins seemed to have no trouble landing the most prestigious commissions from major national institutions of every kind: Glyndebourne Opera, the Victoria and Albert Museum, British Rail, London Transport, the Inland Revenue, even Parliament itself. If he did not have much work abroad it was mainly because he didn't need it.

Hopkins has deployed all the conceptual principles and formal devices he has developed over 20 years of building in his recent unbuilt projects. Truth to materials, modern technology, responsiveness to context, historical awareness, symmetry, circular plan forms, in-between spaces, fabric structures: all appear in different combinations, synthesised into a distinctive, mature style. The style is represented most clearly by three London projects: the New Parliamentary Building, Tottenham Court Road Station Redevelopment and Marylebone Gate Office Development. Like Bracken House they are all unified, basically rectangular forms on the scale of complete urban blocks with five or six-storey facades and either a central courtyard or an atrium, circular in the case of Marylebone Gate. The plans are wholly rational. Internal spaces and circulation routes are organised with diagrammatic clarity around axes of symmetry. This applies even to the complex interweaving of public and private space in the Tottenham Court Road scheme, in which the main axes are diagonal.

All of these buildings have rounded corners, which at Tottenham Court Road and the New Parliamentary Building are developed into turrets. This curious feature is such a characteristic motif in Hopkins' most recent projects that it is worth examining it in some detail. Where does it come from and what prompts its use: perhaps there are historical precedents – English castles, French chateaux, German Romanesque cathedrals? These days Hopkins admits that his attitude to architectural history is that of the 'plundering barbarian' but the spoils are usually closer to home, often on the site next door or even on the site itself. Looking again at the south wing of Bracken House we find that the Classicist Richardson has graced the corners with a pair of unclassical

Above, New Square,
Bedfont Lakes, Heathrow,
Middlesex, 1992.
Right, Mies van der Rohe:
Crown Hall, Illinois
Institute of Technology,
Chicago, 1956.

semicircular turrets. To the north of the New Parliamentary Building stands the castle-like mass of the Norman Shaw Buildings – with corner turrets. The acknowledged inspiration of the plan of Tottenham Court Road is nearby Sicilian Avenue, a diagonal pedestrian short cut defined by a triangular corner block – with corner turrets. But we don't even have to go that far. Right next door, on the other side of Sutton Place, stands a Victorian building with a corner turret.

In fact the corner turret is a common feature of the street architecture of central London. Its appearance in Hopkins' designs signals a willingness to reinforce rather than disrupt the traditional urban pattern. But does it have any functional justification? Apparently not. In the Tottenham Court Road scheme, for example, the turrets house three different functions: mechanical plant, circular conference rooms and, in the main turret on the corner of Oxford Street and Charing Cross Road, a continuous helical ramp intended to be used as a public art gallery. As in the early High-Tech buildings, the relationship between form and function is a loose one. But whereas in those buildings the form is dictated by the demands of a rational structure and an economical enclosing envelope, in these new projects it is dictated by the urban context. But the turret has another meaning. It is a static form, a full stop at the end of a facade, a definition of a boundary; it is the opposite of the indeterminate, infinitely extendible forms of Hopkins' early, out-of-town buildings.

This new, monumental quality is most apparent in another central London project: the proposed redevelopment of the site in front of Victoria Station. Like Hopkins' Tottenham Court Road Station project, the scheme is based on the reorganisation of a complex transport interchange but its most prominent feature is a tall office block with a teardrop-shaped plan and cutaway profile. Here, symmetry is more than just a convenient ordering device. The axis aligns with Victoria Street, so that the building terminates this major thoroughfare.

But even when designing out of town, Hopkins now prefers to use unified, static forms. At Glyndebourne it would probably have been impossible anyway to house the essentially focused

Right, Norman Shaw: North Building, Westminster, London, 1890.
Far right, New Parliamentary Building, Westminster, London, 1989–.

space of an opera auditorium in a factory shed, but the pure oval plan-form of the scheme still comes as a surprise. Like the Fleet Velmead school, it accommodates a wide range of spaces and patterns of use in a single envelope but, instead of a plain rectangle with a lightweight, repetitive structure, there is a solid, permanent, rounded object, rooted in the landscape. The circular, raised roof over the auditorium is clearly a larger version of Hathersage and the materials are also similar. Once again the architectural details reflect the structural characteristics of the materials. The external walls have loadbearing piers, which taper upwards as the load diminishes, and the masonry panels between the piers are supported on true flat arches.

This form of external wall appears again in the last and most important of the unbuilt schemes, the proposed New Inland Revenue Centre in Nottingham. Here Hopkins is not simply fitting into a context, but planning a whole urban quarter. Even at this scale, the plan is basically symmetrical, with traditional corridor streets on a radial pattern focused on the castle hill in the city centre. Each urban block is like a broader, lower version of the proposed central-London buildings, complete with corner turrets. But in the Nottingham scheme the corner turrets have a very definite function, apart from their contribution to the townscape. They house the fire-escape staircases but, more importantly, they also act as ventilation shafts. The proposed

Above, Tottenham Court
Road Station
Redevelopment, 1990–.
Far right, Sicilian Avenue,
Holborn, London.

New Parliamentary Building also incorporates chimney-like air ducts to promote natural ventilation, but their architectural role is secondary. At Nottingham they have become the anchor points of the composition. It is as if the turrets have found their true purpose, with form and function at last combined in a single, satisfying architectural form. They are the latest incarnation of the in-between space idea.

The importance of the Inland Revenue scheme is the way that it gives architectural expression to new environmental concerns. Five years earlier a brief like this would probably have resulted in a series of steel-framed, lightweight-clad, deep-planned, air-conditioned office blocks. That was the 1980s' formula, represented in Hopkins' work by New Square at Bedfont Lakes. But the energy- and pollution-conscious 1990s have led a few forward-looking architects to look again at shallow-planned, naturally lit and naturally ventilated buildings.

Computerised environmental assessments now allow engineers and architects to achieve the right comfort conditions without resorting to energy-squandering mechanical systems.

For Hopkins this is an exciting challenge. He has always seen his architecture as more a practical discipline than a formalistic art. He needs a problem to solve; the more difficult the problem, the better the architecture. What he seeks is an organic relationship between his architecture and the conditions in which it is produced. In the early buildings, that meant giving clear expression to industrial production. In the city-centre projects, it meant responding positively to context. When this seemed to call for the use of more traditional materials, the architecture became the honest expression of the nature of those materials. On the way, he has deliberately extended his repertoire to include compositional devices like symmetry, centredness and monumentality, opening up his architecture to the lessons of the past. In the Inland Revenue scheme everything he has learned has been applied to the solution of a new problem: diminishing resources and increasing pollution. The result has many traditional architectural virtues but is fresh and new. The mature phase in the development of Hopkins' architecture is only just beginning.

Hopkins House, 1975–1976

In designing this building, Michael and Patty Hopkins intended to provide themselves not just with a home and an office for their recently established practice, but also to try out on a small scale the techniques they were developing for larger, commercial buildings. The house was to be built from metal and glass components, put together in the simplest possible way. It was to make no conventional architectural concessions to its context – a well-established street of Georgian and Regency villas in Hampstead, London. Its 'footprint' was defined by the front and back building lines and by the site boundaries on either side, leaving metre-wide clear strips to avoid the legal complications of party walls. This produced a 10 metre by 12 metre rectangle. The building had to be two storeys high in order to provide the required floor area. From the front, however, it appears to be a single-storey building because most of the site is 3 metres below road level. The main entrance, therefore, is at first-floor level, reached via a footbridge, which spans the steep slope that falls from the back edge of the pavement.

Once the basic form of the building and the access were established, the next step was to devise a suitable structural system. A small-scale structural grid, 4 metres by 2 metres, was chosen. This obviated the need for any secondary structure and meant the structural components could be very small and light. Perimeter columns at 2 metre centres support cladding and glazing without sheeting rails or sub-frames.

This basic strategy has produced a building of extreme simplicity and refinement. Troughed metal decking for both the floor and the roof is supported on a two-way grid of lattice trusses on 60mm, square steel columns. Joints are usually welded and the detailing is simple and repetitive. Side walls are of insulated, profiled metal sheeting; front and back walls are assembled entirely from full-height, horizontally sliding glass panels with no vertical frames. There are no ceilings or wall linings. Partitions are made of prefabricated melamine-faced panels. Other internal finishes are the metal and glass of the external walls and the carpeted floors.

The internal planning is surprisingly open and flexible; domestic spaces are mainly on the ground floor, with the former studio at entrance level, the two being connected by an open spiral staircase. Solid partitions were designed to fit the basic frame, but in practice it has been found that in most cases free-hanging venetian blinds are sufficient to define the various functions. Heating is by a direct gas-fired warm-air furnace with only one outlet on the top floor. Ductwork extends into individual rooms on the ground floor. Extremes of heat gain and heat loss through the all-glass walls are moderated by internal venetian blinds and up to 50 per cent of the glazing can be opened.

Section and floor plans
1 footbridge
2 entrance
3 studio
4 shower room
5 bed
6 dressing
7 sitting
8 kitchen
9 dining
10 street
11 garden

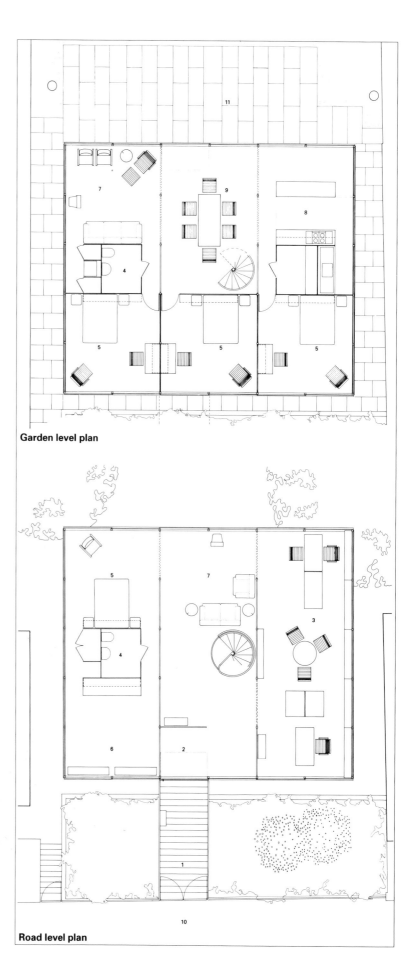

Garden level plan

Road level plan

Location plan

Within the design parameters established by Michael and Patty Hopkins, their house, in its strategic form, 'designed itself'. The building zone is defined by the street and garden building lines, which are just over 10 metres apart. At the sides the house is pulled back 1 metre from the adjoining buildings to avoid any party-wall conditions. The house is two storeys high; one floor, originally the Hopkinses' office, is entered at street level, and the other at garden level beneath.

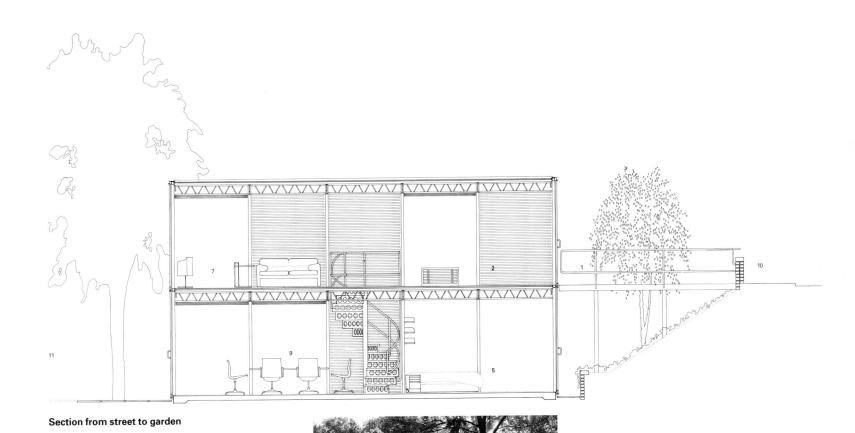

Section from street to garden

Behind the house's glass facades, aluminium venetian blinds give an impression of opacity from outside that is absent from the interior, where one is conscious of the apparently all-surrounding glass and the extraordinary lightness that this generates.

The house was a test-bed
for techniques developed
for larger buildings:
structural members are
small and repetitive;
floors and walls are thin
membranes and are
expressed as such;
perimeter columns are
used directly as cladding
and glazing supports.

The Hopkins House has few internal partitions or doors; the divisions between spaces are formed by the minimalist intervention of venetian blinds of the type used around the perimeter.

Greene King Draught Beer Cellars, 1977–1980

'Racking' is the brewer's term for filling casks with beer. For as long as anyone at Greene King could remember, this process had been carried out at the company's Westgate site in Bury St Edmunds, Suffolk. Access to this site was poor, however, and with the increasing popularity of draught beers in the 1970s, the old cellars had become inadequate. In any case, the site had been earmarked for a new fermenting block. In 1977 Hopkins was commissioned to design a new racking plant on a neighbouring site so that beer could be delivered to the new building via a pipeline from the old brewery building.

Although closely tailored to the special functional requirements of the racking process, the single-storey building is simple, unified and rectangular both on plan and in section. Its concrete floor is raised off the ground on short columns to protect it from the occasional flooding of the nearby River Linnett. However, setting the whole working plane at lorry tailgate-height also simplified the design of the full-width loading and unloading bays at either end of the building.

A steel superstructure of lattice trusses on three rows of tubular columns supports a flat roof, which is cantilevered out over the loading bays. Shorter cantilevers along the sides of the building allow the columns to be set back from the external walls, creating full-length corridors, which end in short flights of external steps down to ground level. The purpose-made welded trusses, with rectangular hollow-section booms and tubular struts, are exposed externally over the loading bays. Side walls are of silver PVF2-coated, profiled steel, lightweight cladding, divided into bays and perforated only by a pair of central exit doors. End walls consist entirely of fully glazed roller shutters opening onto the loading bays.

Internally, small freestanding buildings-within-a-building house ancillary functions such as mess rooms, wcs, offices, workshops and plant. A larger enclosure, occupying a whole structural bay, serves as a cool store. The remainder of the space houses the beer-storage vessels and machinery for washing, filling and loading the casks. Provision is made for possible future expansion by adding a third structural bay to the side of the building, thus preserving the logical, linear progression of the process.

In essence this is a very simple building. But the refinement of its proportions and detailing set it apart from the hundreds of steel-clad, portal-framed sheds that sprang up on industrial estates all over the country in the late 1970s: the raised floor, cantilevered at the edges in order to create the illusion that the building is hovering above its site, the panelled side walls of horizontally rather than vertically profiled steel sheet, and the elegant cantilevered porticoes over the loading bays combine to give it a dignified architectural bearing, which belies its mundane function.

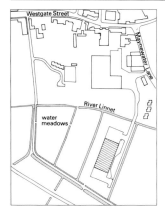

Location plan

The building's internal
layout perfectly describes
the linear process that
it contains: dray lorries
deliver empty casks
at one end of the building
and collect full ones at
the other end, each cask
having been through
washing, filling
and storage stages
in between.

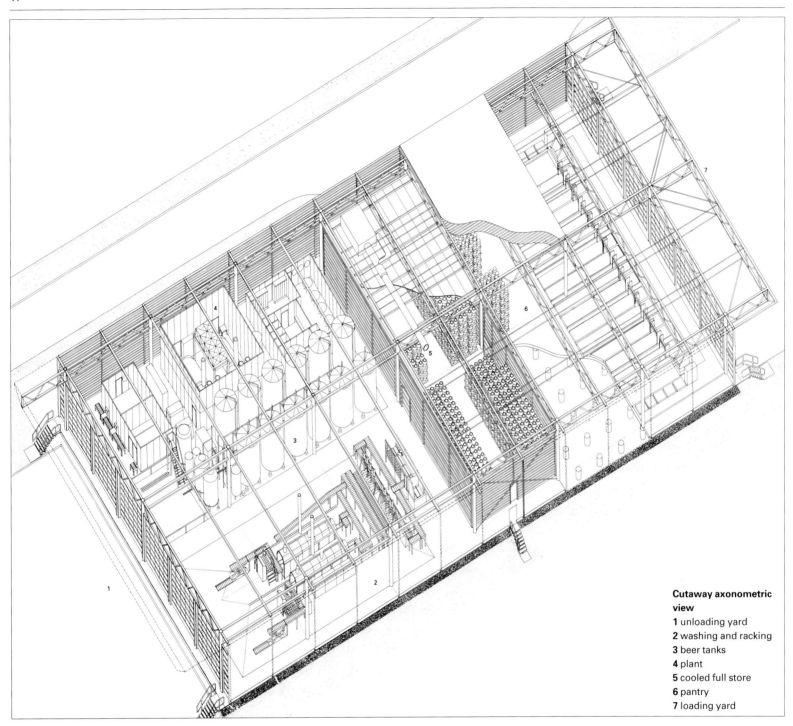

Cutaway axonometric view
1 unloading yard
2 washing and racking
3 beer tanks
4 plant
5 cooled full store
6 pantry
7 loading yard

Long section through building and loading yards

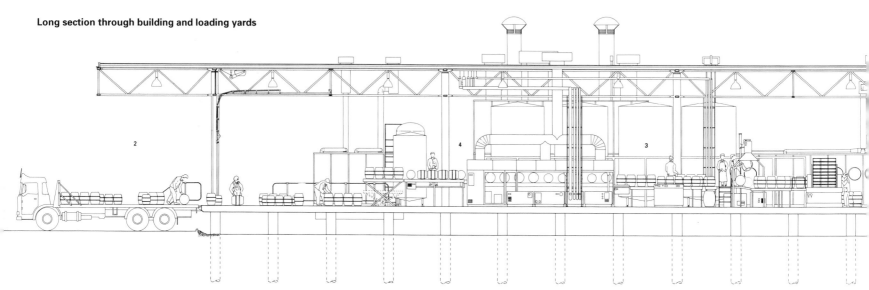

Beer arrives at the racking plant by overhead pipeline from the Greene King brewery. The building and the process it contains are so finely matched that the whole organisation achieves a machine-like order and clarity.

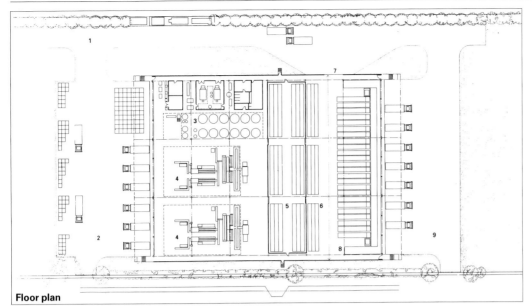

**Floor plan and
long section**
1 access road
2 unloading yard
3 beer tanks
4 washing and racking
5 cooled full store
6 kegs
7 keg unloading bay
8 pantry
9 loading yard

Floor plan

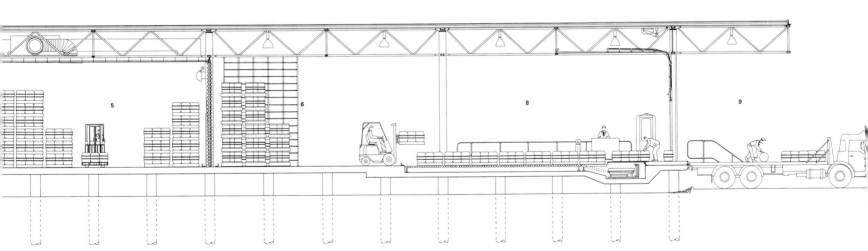

Owing to its location on
a river flood plain, the
building is raised above
the ground, its floor
level corresponding with
the loading height of
a brewery dray lorry.
While clearly functionally
advantageous, elevating
the building in this way
gives it an added degree
of poise and elegance.

Patera Building System, 1980 – 1982

Patera was conceived not as a single building but as a building system. The client, Nigel Dale, perceived a demand for small, standardised, single-storey buildings, suitable for industrial or office use, which could be made as kits, delivered to the site in containers and erected quickly with minimal plant. For Hopkins this was the opportunity to realise one of the ideals of modern architecture: the building that is mass-produced in a factory, just like a car. The closeness of the relationship between designer and component manufacturer produced a building of unusual technical refinement and accuracy. A full-size prototype was built alongside the factory so that every element of the structure could be tested and changes could be made if necessary.

The prototype building is a simple box, with a wraparound steel envelope and glazed gable ends. The floor area is 216 square metres and the internal height greater than 3.5 metres, which is high enough for most light-industrial uses but not high enough to permit the introduction of a mezzanine floor.

The structure is a tubular-steel lattice frame, placed outside the external envelope of the building. This reduces the extent of the envelope and of the space enclosed, with consequent savings in materials and running costs. More importantly, it obviates the need for fireproofing. The usual disadvantage of an external frame is that the top boom of the roof truss is unrestrained and liable to buckle. In a Patera building, this problem is solved in an ingenious way. What appear at first to be trusses supported on lattice uprights are in fact three-pin portal frames. The top booms are connected in the centre of the span by a special, hinged rod capable of withstanding only tensile stress. This effectively converts the three-pin structure into a two-pin structure whenever wind loading causes an uplift on the roof.

A remarkable feature of the external envelope is that the same type of panel is used for the walls and the roof. Each panel is a sandwich of mineral-fibre insulation between two skins of ribbed, pressed steel, supported by rectangular hollow-section purlins. Joints between the panels, in both walls and roof, are sealed by gaskets. Wiring and water pipes are accommodated in ducts within the thickness of the wall. All of the prefabricated components are small enough to be packed into a standard container and handled on site by a fork-lift truck. Assembly of the complete kit on a prepared concrete ground slab takes only 10 days.

The Hopkins office in Marylebone is accommodated in a slightly larger version of the standard Patera building. The most obvious differences are that the height has been increased to allow the insertion of a mezzanine floor, glazing has been introduced in the roof, and the portal-frame structure has been replaced by ordinary trusses on simple tubular-steel columns.

Four prototype Patera units were erected on an industrial estate in Stoke on Trent; typically, each unit took three men 10 working days to complete, a fork-lift truck being the only special piece of equipment required on site. Speed was part of the system's attraction: Patera set out to tackle the traditionally time-consuming aspects of the building process. The initial phases of site preparation and slab construction were organised conventionally, while the final stage of fitting out was left to the individual purchaser. Hopkins argued that most organisations wait until the last minute before commissioning a building and then want it as soon as possible, and because this middle phase is where the major investment lies, that is where saving time can really pay dividends.

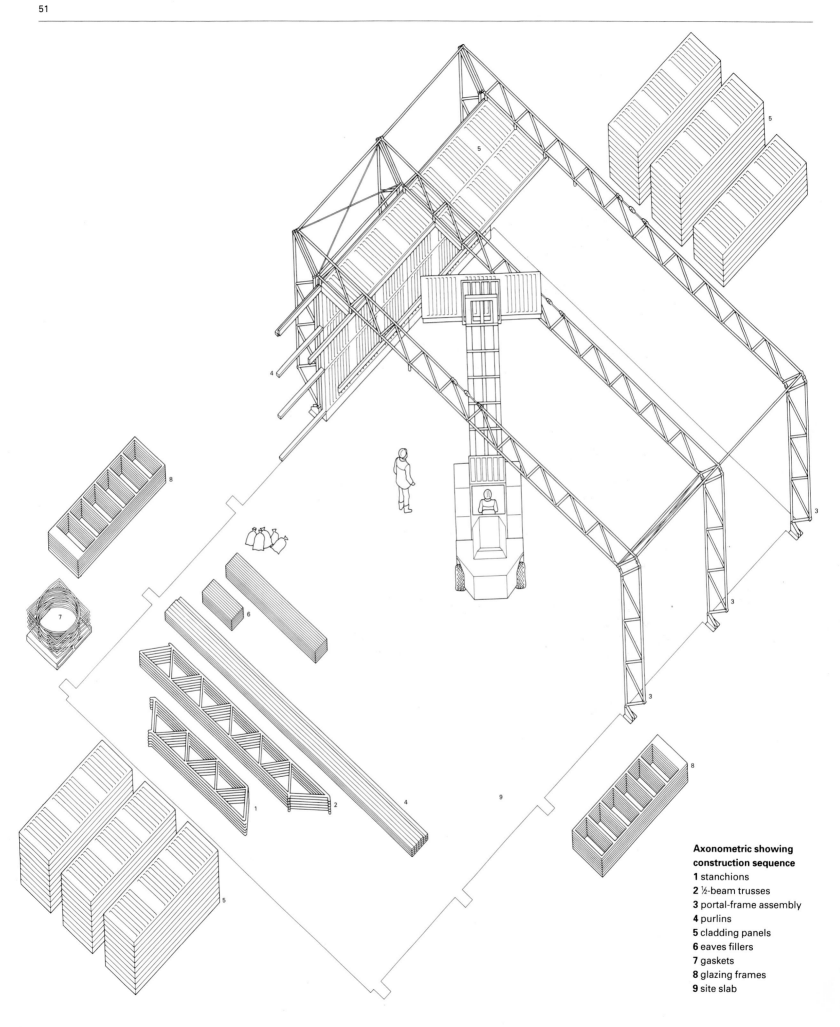

**Axonometric showing
construction sequence**
1 stanchions
2 ½-beam trusses
3 portal-frame assembly
4 purlins
5 cladding panels
6 eaves fillers
7 gaskets
8 glazing frames
9 site slab

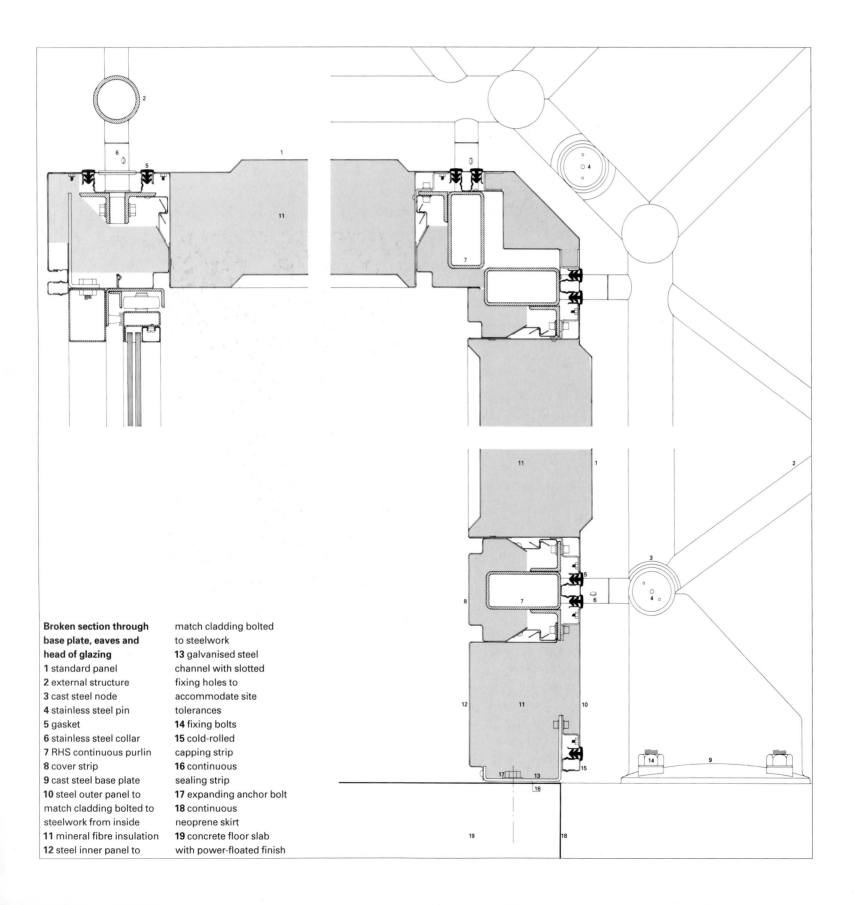

Broken section through base plate, eaves and head of glazing

1 standard panel
2 external structure
3 cast steel node
4 stainless steel pin
5 gasket
6 stainless steel collar
7 RHS continuous purlin
8 cover strip
9 cast steel base plate
10 steel outer panel to match cladding bolted to steelwork from inside
11 mineral fibre insulation
12 steel inner panel to match cladding bolted to steelwork
13 galvanised steel channel with slotted fixing holes to accommodate site tolerances
14 fixing bolts
15 cold-rolled capping strip
16 continuous sealing strip
17 expanding anchor bolt
18 continuous neoprene skirt
19 concrete floor slab with power-floated finish

Patera's components were all factory-made to a high degree of accuracy; the on-site process was simply one of assembly. Joints between panels were sealed with neoprene gaskets, the same detail being applied to the roof as to the walls.

One of two Patera units
constructed at Canary
Wharf, London, in 1985
allowed refinement of
the system to continue.
As with the earlier units,
an exoskeletal frame
protects the structure
from a fire within
the building and allows
member sizes to be
kept to a minimum.

**Ground floor plan of
the Hopkins office**
1 reception
2 main studio
3 meeting
4 kitchen
5 plant
6 wcs
7 print room
8 glazed link
9 new studio
10 model shop
11 store

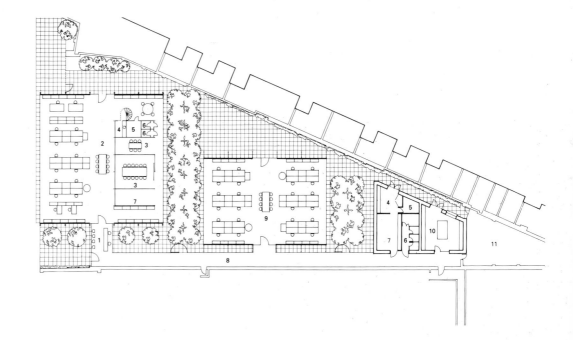

Location plan

Michael and Patty
Hopkins' own office in
Marylebone, is a further
stage in the Patera story;
double height, with a
freestanding service
core and mezzanine, it
has glazed panels in
the walls and the roof.
An earlier prototype
has been acquired as
an annexe.

Schlumberger Cambridge Research Centre 1982–1992

Phase One, 1982–85

This building, on a greenfield site just outside Cambridge, is a centre for research into aspects of oil exploration, including drilling and fluid mechanics, rock and well-bore physics, and computer modelling of drilling information. The client's brief envisaged four main types of accommodation: laboratories, individual offices for scientists, a drilling-rig testing station and staff recreation space. Normally in a building of this kind the noisy, dirty activities of the testing station would be placed well away from the other functions. However, the client was keen to promote easy communication between scientists in all departments, including those working in the testing station, and this seemed to call for a more integrated design. Hopkins' solution was a bold one: to put the testing station right in the heart of the building where it could be overlooked by the other laboratories.

The basic concept is simple. Two long single-storey wings, placed parallel to each other 24 metres apart, house the laboratories, facing inwards, and the individual scientists' rooms, facing outwards. Each wing is divided into five sections, articulated by recessed entrances. These sections have some superficial similarities to the standard Patera buildings developed by Hopkins with Nigel Dale. The details, however, are different. External, lattice roof trusses are supported on tubular-steel columns. Flat roofs are fairly conventional, with a continuous waterproof membrane on an insulated metal deck. Flank walls are of profiled steel but the main external walls consist entirely of full-height sliding glass doors.

In between the parallel wings a billowing fabric structure like a three-ring circus tent covers the drilling-rig testing station and the main social space known as the winter garden. The fabric is Teflon-coated glass fibre – the first large-scale use of this material in Britain. It is uninsulated and transmits about 13 per cent of daylight. The large-scale spaces, therefore, have a quasi-external character, though the winter garden includes a restaurant and a library as well as the main reception area. A cat's-cradle of cables transmits the weight of the fabric to the ground via four suspension bridge-like structures. These line up with the recessed entrances in the side wings, reaching over them to anchors in the ground beyond. Two separate structural systems – one for the large spans of the testing station and winter garden, the other for the short spans of the office and laboratory wings – are thus interlocked.

Services are mostly accommodated below floor level. The air-conditioned laboratories are provided with undercrofts to house air-handling equipment and other plant, while electrical and data services are carried in the troughs of the steel-decked suspended floors.

The main equipment in the testing station comprises three drilling test pits up to 20 metres deep, an underground high-pressure pump chamber and a 10 tonne gantry crane covering the entire floor area, with a maximum hook height of 10 metres. The adjacent laboratories are acoustically insulated by 21mm thick, laminated glass units.

Phase Two, 1990–92

One way to extend the original Schlumberger building in Cambridge would have been simply to add more bays to the essentially linear plan. Changes in research methods meant, however, that the quasi-external testing station was no longer central to the building's function. More offices and laboratories were required, but these could be located satisfactorily in a separate building. This led the Hopkins team to conceive a masterplan for the whole site based on the campus model. The new building would be the first step in the new strategy.

Although the new building is separate, it nevertheless has a strong formal relationship with the original building. Two virtually identical pavilions are placed one on either side of the main axis, or 'broadwalk', which connects the site entrance and car park to the original building. A top-lit atrium bridges over the broadwalk, linking the two pavilions and forming the entrance hall and reception area for the whole complex. Each pavilion, two storeys high and square on plan, is clearly a development of the design of the Solid State Logic building

near Oxford, except that the double-height central space has been replaced by laboratories, plant rooms, a computer suite and a conference room. As at Solid State Logic, the first floor overhangs the ground floor all the way round, the external walls are totally glazed with external venetian blinds at the upper level, and the concrete first-floor slab is supported on tubular-steel columns.

There are, however, a number of important technical innovations. Instead of ordinary in-situ concrete, the first-floor slab is a composite structure of prefabricated ferro-concrete permanent formwork with an in-situ topping. The formwork is made from a thin sand and cement mortar sprayed onto a light steel mesh formed in a complex mould. The curved profiles of the mould conform approximately to the stresses in the structure, creating a pattern on the exposed soffit that recalls Pier Luigi Nervi's 1954 Gatti Wool Factory in Rome. There are no suspended ceilings. Light fittings and air grilles are cast into the slab and horizontal services are accommodated in a raised floor above.

The roof structure also differs from

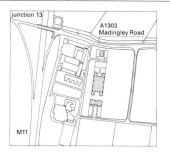

Location plan

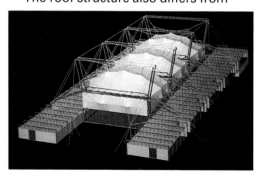

Computer modelling was used as a design tool by the building's engineers, whose development work on the fabric roof enclosure and supporting structure was fundamental to the formal resolution of the building. The freestanding building that constitutes Schlumberger's second phase, opposite, appears as a pair of gate houses in front of the original pavilion underlining the axiality of the scheme on the site and reinforcing the notion of Schlumberger as an embryonic campus development.

that at Begbroke. The lattice space deck is replaced by a grillage of steel beams on a 3.6 metre, square module. These are connected by means of specially designed cruciform castings of spheroidal graphite iron – a material that is almost as strong as steel but easier to cast. The grillage supports a flat deck of stressed-skin plywood panels. Again the structure is exposed, with no suspended ceiling, and the light fittings are recessed into the deck.

The third technical innovation is in the fabric roofs that cover the atrium and the small meeting areas in the corners of each pavilion. Unlike the big tent of the original building, which is suspended from an exposed steel structure, these roofs are supported pneumatically. Each structural bay is covered by an inflated cushion formed from three layers of transparent fluorocarbon film, welded to gaskets fitted to aluminium extrusions. Dried air is introduced into the building through a slot in the aluminium section and automatically topped up when required.

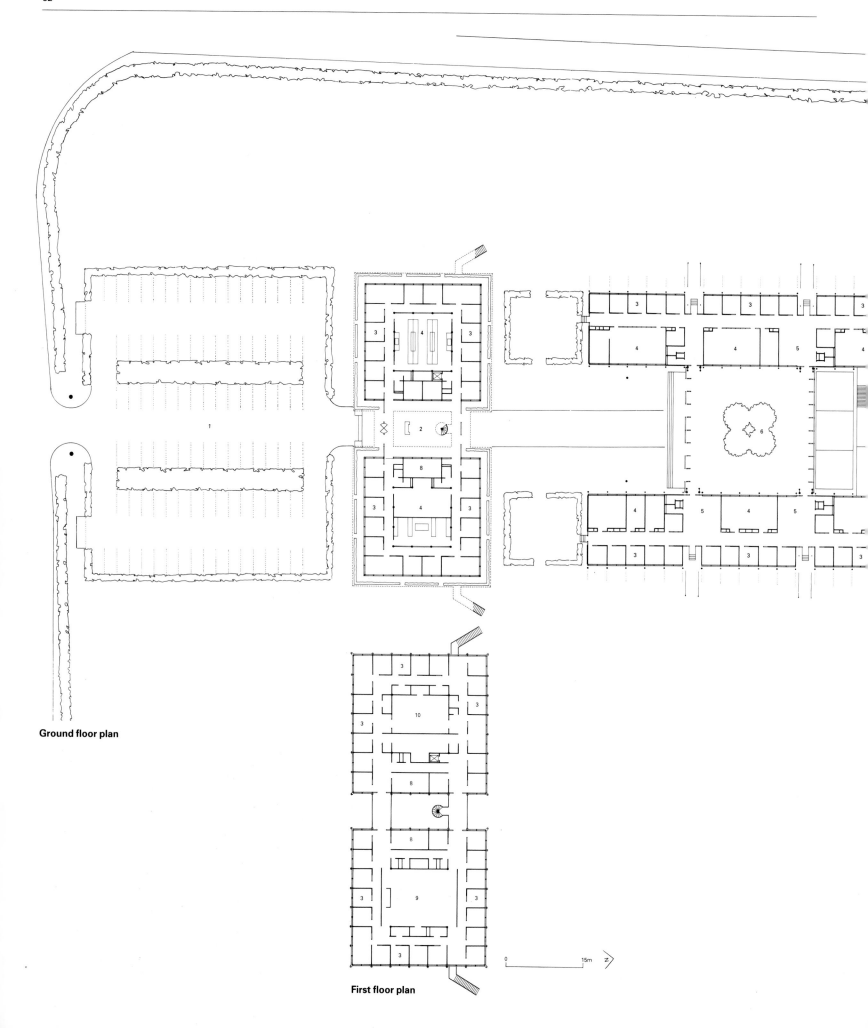

Ground floor plan

First floor plan

0   15m   Z

63

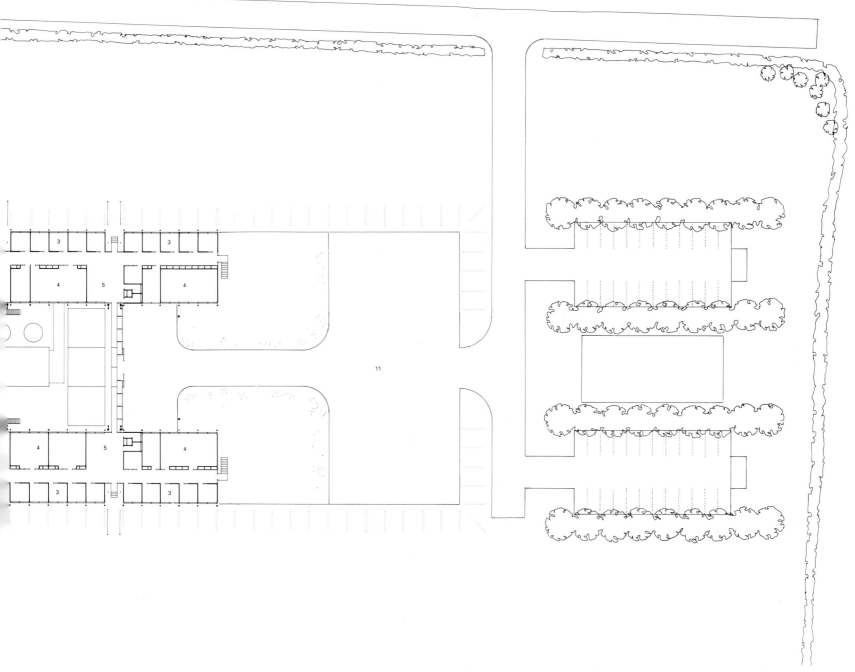

Floor plans

1 car parking
2 entrance hall
3 scientist's study
4 laboratories
5 discussion area
6 winter garden
7 test station
8 meeting
9 conference
10 computer
11 service yard

Hopkins' Schlumberger development has expanded as an embryonic campus. The most recent element in this process, the reception building, takes few architectural clues from the test-station block. It provides additional scientists' rooms, laboratories, computer and conference rooms along with a relocated administration department. The scientists' rooms, which line the perimeter on both levels of the new building, follow the original 3.6 metre planning module, thus maintaining the space standards that Schlumberger considers appropriate, while forming an element of visual unity between the two structures in the rhythm and detail of their external envelopes; the full-height glazing, which features strongly in the new building, has been carried over directly from the earlier building's office wings.

At night, the test-station
building becomes
transparent, its pupae-like
fabric roof glowing
mysteriously on the flat
Cambridgeshire skyline
to form an intriguing local
landmark.

The winter garden, which
forms a restaurant and
social space for
Schlumberger staff,
is divided from the
experimental forum of
the test station by a great
glass wall, which allows
clear views along the full
length of the building.

Like its formative predecessor, the Solid State Logic building, the first-floor slabs of the Schlumberger reception building cantilever out to shade the ground floor; this gesture also reduces the building's apparent mass. The roofline was kept deliberately low to achieve a balanced relationship with the earlier building. In part, this was achieved by keeping the floor-to-ceiling heights to a minimum but the site's falling contours were also used to advantage allowing the reception building to sit 600mm below the datum of the winter-garden floor.

74

Schlumberger's test station gives the centre its practical experimental focus although the company's research interests are increasingly centred on computer-based models and data sources, which have reduced the importance of the test station's drilling-simulation facilities.

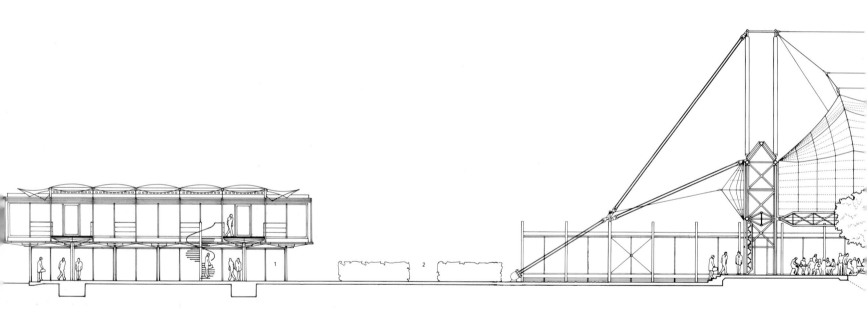

Long section through site
1 entrance hall
2 courtyard
3 winter garden
4 drilling test pits
5 test station
6 service yard

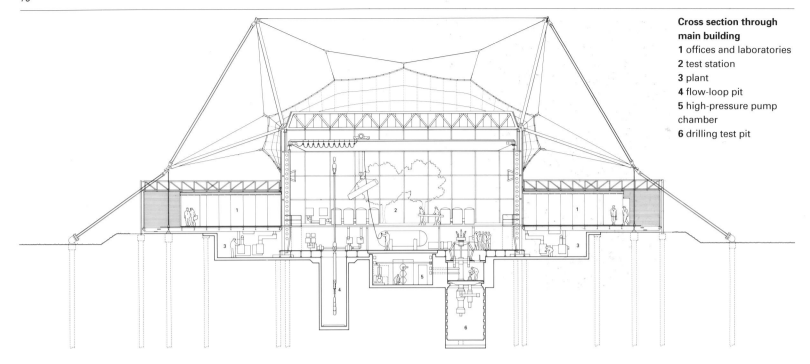

Cross section through main building
1 offices and laboratories
2 test station
3 plant
4 flow-loop pit
5 high-pressure pump chamber
6 drilling test pit

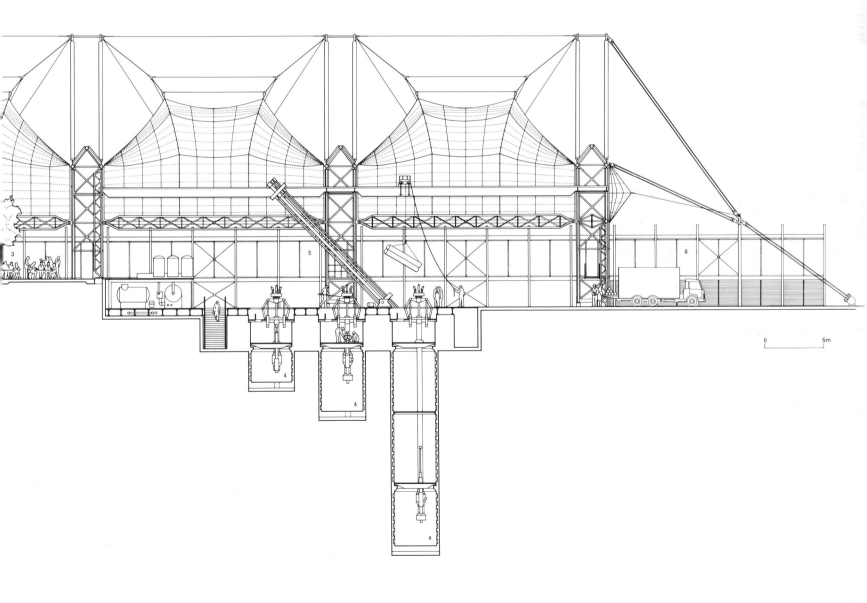

The Schlumberger
reception building's
coffered and cantilevered
first-floor slab is far more
expressive than anything
seen before in Hopkins'
work. On the first floor,
the columns sit on
finger like projections
in the slab.

Fleet Velmead Infants School, 1984–1986

Hampshire County Council's reputation as a patron of fine architecture is legendary. In 1984 the council's chief architect, Colin Stansfield Smith, asked Hopkins to design a replacement for a crumbling Victorian infants school at Fleet. The resulting design was revolutionary. Hopkins proposed an open-plan building entirely roofed by a tent structure, using the stretched-fabric technology that the practice was then developing with engineers Buro Happold. Development of the design reached an advanced stage but was finally rejected for being too innovative by the council's education committee. The tent structure was abandoned, but the basic idea of a flexible plan beneath a single roof survived.

Fleet Velmead Infants School has a plain rectangular plan, divided in two by a top-lit circulation spine, with cellular spaces, including the main hall, on the north side and a row of identical open-plan classrooms on the south side. As always in a Hopkins building the basic structure is simple and honestly expressed. A barn-like, kinked, double-pitched roof of insulated metal decking, with glazing at the ridge over the circulation spine, is supported by a lightweight steel frame. This frame is pecisely detailed and highly refined. Tubular compression members and diagonal bracing rods are fixed together with flanges and pins, all clearly visible. The components have been designed to enhance their apparent slenderness.

Main rafters, for example, are mostly concealed in the depth of the roof decking, with only the tubular bottom booms exposed beneath the soffit. These are cut short at the external wall and at the columns that straddle the spine so they appear to float, unsupported. Similarly, the slenderness of the perimeter columns is enhanced by their dumb-bell profile, with tubular booms on either side of the glass external wall.

Within this simple envelope, cellular spaces take the form of structurally separate enclosures, 4.5 metres high. The main roof oversails these enclosures on the north side, with air-handling plant installed in the space between the ceiling and the roof. On the south side, with the exception of small octagonal quiet areas, the classrooms are open to the soffit of the main roof and to the top-lit spine. This creates a pleasant, airy quality of daylight, despite the relatively deep plan. Heating is by hot-water pipes cast into the floor screed – a sensible system in a building for children.

The south wall is entirely glazed and each classroom has a wide, double door that opens onto a paved terrace so that the children can play outside. Beyond the terrace the landscape is wild and boggy and is itself a valuable teaching tool. The original fabric structure proposal survives in a fragmentary form in the awnings that shade the south wall and give the building an appropriately playful character.

Location plan

All of Fleet Velmead's classrooms open out onto paved play areas where a great deal of teaching activity takes place in the summer months. Protective awnings screen the fully glazed elevation from the unwanted effects of glare and solar gain.

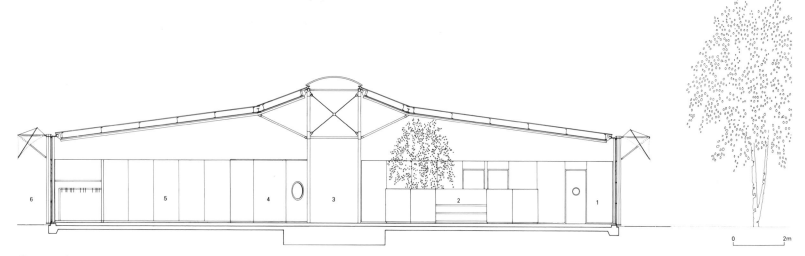

Cross section through school
1 entrance
2 resource area
3 circulation spine
4 quiet area
5 classroom
6 paved play area

0   2m

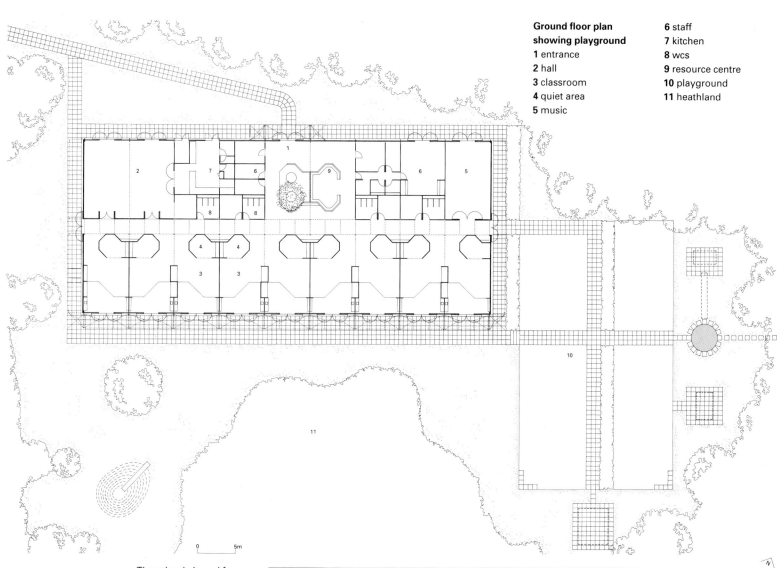

Ground floor plan showing playground
1 entrance
2 hall
3 classroom
4 quiet area
5 music
6 staff
7 kitchen
8 wcs
9 resource centre
10 playground
11 heathland

0   5m

The school viewed from the south; the wild, boggy landscape that meets the building has been left untouched and is valued by staff as a convenient natural teaching resource.

Each open-plan classroom has access to a quiet room conceived as a small 'house', which is acoustically effective even without doors. Porthole windows placed at child's-eye level allow views in and out of these rooms, maintaining visual contact across the plan.

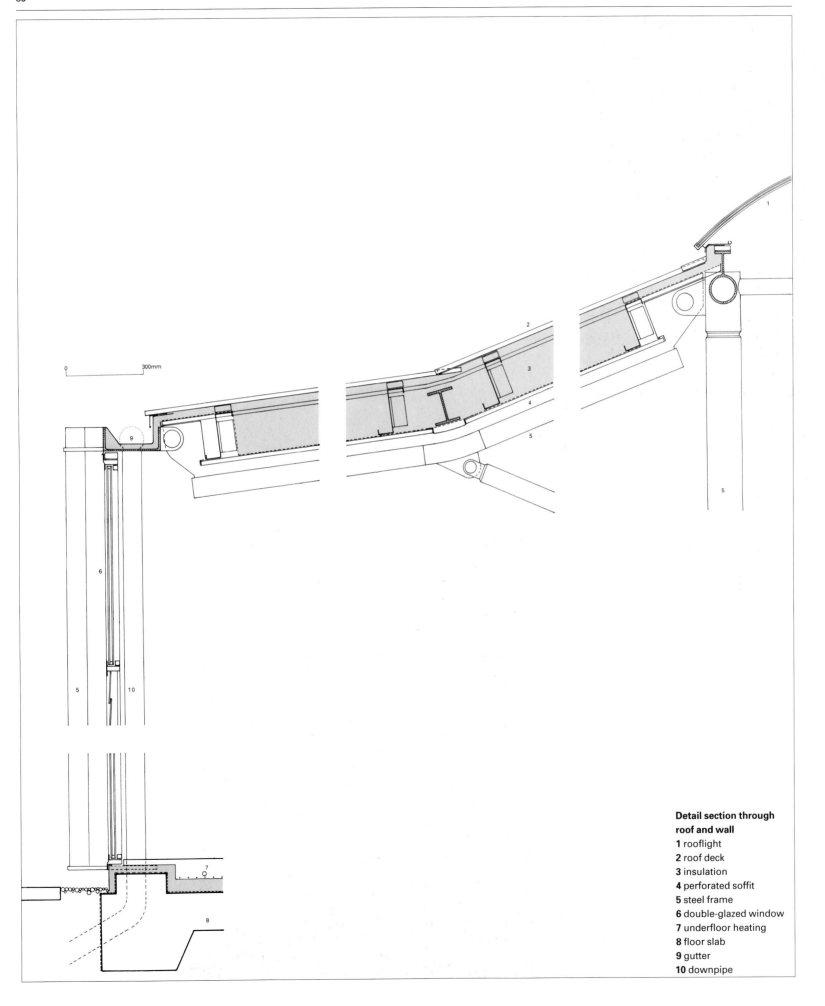

0   300mm

Detail section through roof and wall
1 rooflight
2 roof deck
3 insulation
4 perforated soffit
5 steel frame
6 double-glazed window
7 underfloor heating
8 floor slab
9 gutter
10 downpipe

The structural solution
for the long glazed
northern and southern
elevations is ingenious; a
double column, forming
a dumb-bell in plan, also
serves as a rainwater
downpipe welded to a
structural gutter section,
which allows the
eaves depth to be
kept to a minimum.

Lord's Cricket Ground 1984–1991

Mound Stand, 1984–87

Lord's is the symbolic home of English cricket. In 1984 the Marylebone Cricket Club in London decided to celebrate Lord's 200th anniversary by rebuilding the old Mound Stand. Five architects were invited to submit proposals. Only Hopkins proposed to retain a part of the original stand, designed by Frank Verity in the 1890s. The reason was more practical than sentimental: it allowed the construction schedule to be conveniently divided into two phases.

Verity's original proposal had been to support the back of the single tier of seating on a brick arcade. In the event, this design was compromised and only part of the arcade was built, the remainder of the seating being supported on an exposed steel frame. In phase one of the Hopkins scheme, carried out in the winter of 1985, the seating tier was renovated, the arcade was extended along the whole length of the stand, as originally intended, and the steel-framed roof was demolished. In phase two, carried out the following winter, a new superstructure was added, including 27 private viewing boxes and a second tier of seating. The superstructure was erected in two months so that the turf, which had been removed, could be relaid in time for the next season.

This superstructure is entirely supported on a single row of six, 400mm diameter steel columns linked by a storey-height plate girder. Lattice girders at 3.66 metre centres cantilever out from the plate girder like ribs from a spine. This forms the skeleton of a three-storey structure hovering over the original tier of seating. Private boxes and dining rooms hang below the skeleton, while service spaces such as tank rooms and wcs occupy the spaces between the ribs. A tier of raked seating backed by open-air restaurants and bars sits on top. The six columns continue upwards to become masts supporting a flamboyant canopy of PVC-coated, polyester fabric. The whole structure is prevented from toppling over by tension members anchored to the ground at the back. These are strapped to the piers of the brick arcade in order to stiffen them and enable them to withstand the occasional compressive stresses caused by wind loading.

As cricket is played only in the summer, the building is unheated and most of the external walls are uninsulated. Materials are generally plain and austere. Private boxes, for example, have sliding and folding, frameless glass doors opening onto the continuous raked balcony facing the wicket, with party walls of fairfaced concrete blockwork and rear walls of glass block to shed borrowed light into the corridor. The external walls of the dining rooms on the other side of the corridor combine frameless glass with glass blocks in full-height panels. On the service floor above, the external wall is formed by a second plate girder, which stiffens the frame. This idea of an all-steel external enclosure is also expressed in the

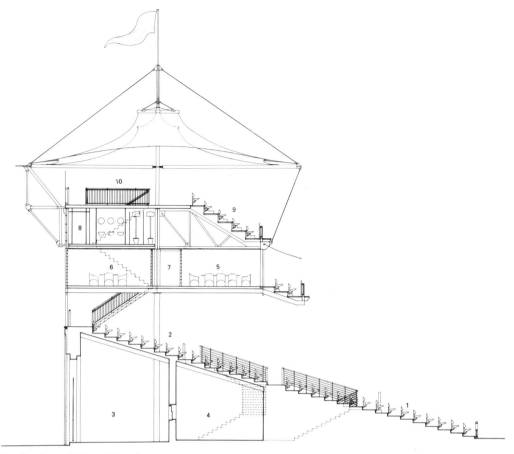

Section through Mound Stand

freestanding lift shaft that plugs into one end of the building.

The Mound Stand is extremely popular among architectural critics and cricket lovers alike. It represents a turning point in the development of Hopkins' architecture. The extension of an existing building in the same style; the use of traditional materials and structural forms; the conscious echoing of the romantic image of the tent by the village green – these were all additions to Hopkins' repertoire.

Two major engineering determinants governed the form of the Mound Stand's superstructure: firstly, columns above terrace level had to be kept to a minimum to avoid obscuring the spectators' view of play; secondly, the superstructure had to be erected in two-months so that the turf could be relaid in time for the next season. Primary structural elements are all in welded steel and centre on a high-level, 2.6 metre-deep plated spine girder that runs along the middle of the plan. This is supported on a row of circular columns.

Compton and Edrich Stands, 1989–91

After the success of the Mound Stand, Hopkins was commissioned to rebuild the stands at the 'nursery end' of the ground. These were designed by Herbert Baker, with the engineer Oscar Faber, in the 1920s. They had fallen into disrepair and were approaching the end of their useful lives.

It was envisaged that the new building would take the same two-tier form but, if possible, with an increased seating capacity. Hopkins' design increases the capacity from 5,000 to 9,000 by encroaching on the unused strip of outfield outside the boundary rope. At the same time the viewing conditions from the lower tier have been improved, minimising the number of seats with restricted vision, and the underside of the upper tier has been raised so that all spectators have a clear view not just of the pitch but also of the scoreboard at the pavilion end. The gap between the two stands is in line with the main test-match pitches so that no spectators are seated behind the bowler's arm where any movement might disturb the batsman's concentration. There is, however, a lightweight steel bridge at a high level between the stands, which serves as a platform for broadcast television cameras.

The structure of the upper tier has been designed to be of minimum depth in order to maintain sight lines while conforming to the client's requirement that the new stands should not restrict the view from the pavilion of trees outside the ground. A curved and inclined in-situ concrete slab forms the compression member of a series of spine trusses with steel booms and struts, balancing on a single row of tubular columns. Secondary, radial, concrete T-beams of different depths are stiffened by steel struts connected to the bottom booms of the trusses. The whole structure is prevented from toppling over by vertical and raking steel columns, which tie the back edge of the slab to the ground.

The arrangement therefore is similar in principle to that of the superstructure of the Mound Stand. Lateral stability is provided by vertical steel-plate girders incorporated in the staircases at the back of the stand. The combination of steel and reinforced concrete is unusual and it makes the most efficient use of the structural characteristics of these materials. Considerable care has been taken in the design of the concrete formwork, with recessed and projecting joints to emphasise the moulded nature of the material.

The simple, low profile forms of the Compton and Edrich Stands may lack the architectural presence of the Mound Stand but the number of extra seats they provide exceeds the total number accommodated in the earlier building. This makes a significant difference to the revenue earning potential of the ground on the eight days in the year when it is full to capacity.

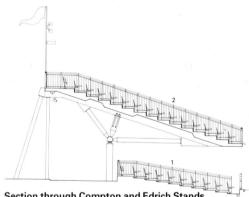

Section through Compton and Edrich Stands

Location plan

**Detail section through
Mound Stand**
1 translucent fabric
roof
2 boundary cable
tensioning assembly
3 transverse cable
4 catenary cable
5 roof-support column
6 steel pick-up ring
7 tie cable
8 roof pick-up cable
9 bar
10 service totem
11 toughened glass
perimeter screen
12 stair balustrade
13 spine beam
14 end bracing frame
15 rib beam

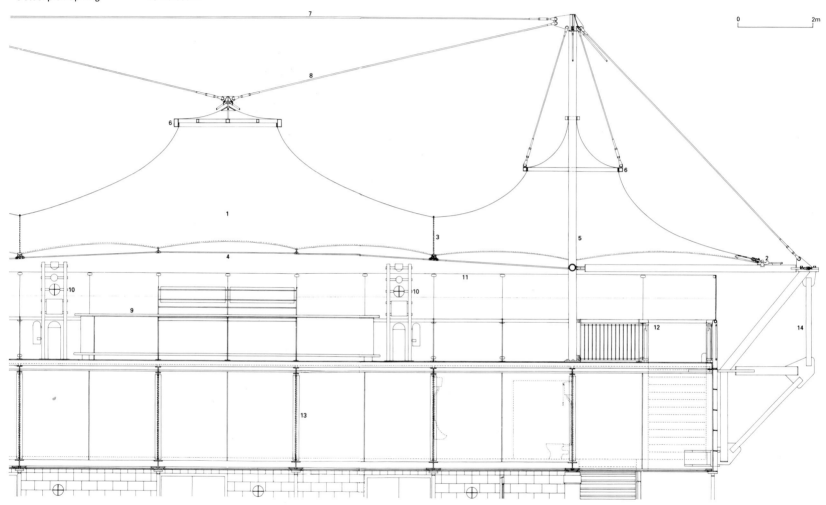

0   2m

The structural solution
for the Mound Stand's
fabric roof relies on six
masts, each extended
from the columns below,
which support truncated
fabric cones with bases
roughly twice the width
of a structural bay. In
between are suspended
a series of larger cones,
which sit higher than
their smaller partners.

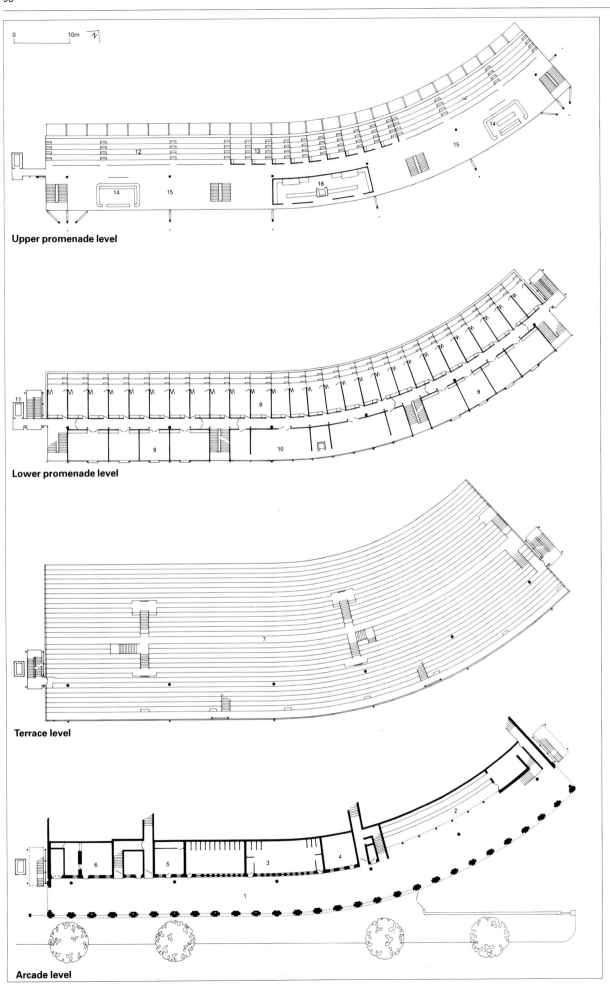

0   10m

Upper promenade level

Lower promenade level

Terrace level

Arcade level

Floor plans
1 arcade
2 arcade bar
3 public wcs
4 shop
5 chief steward
6 police
7 terrace seating
8 private boxes
9 private dining room
10 kitchens
11 lift
12 debenture seating
13 private viewing boxes
14 upper-level bar
15 restaurant
16 servery

Essentially a temperate
building, the Mound
Stand is not intended
to provide a complete
enclosure; the
upper deck, beneath
the fabric roof, has a
quintessentially English,
marquee-like character,
creating the illusion
that Lord's is once again
a village green.

The Mound Stand's structural systems lighten as they rise skyward, from the heavy earthiness of the brick arcades, through the plated steel and glass block of the superstructure to the thin membrane of the roof, which caps the whole composition.

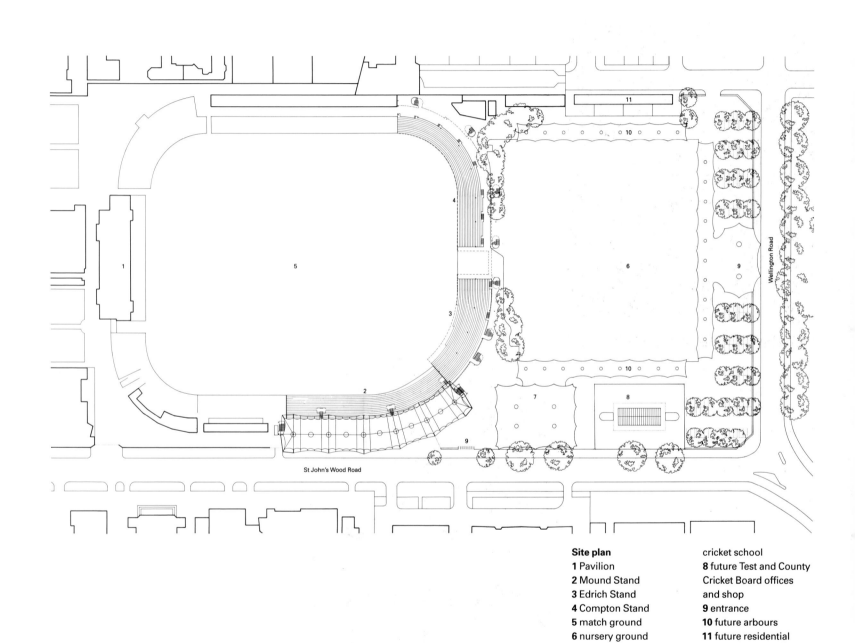

Site plan
1 Pavilion
2 Mound Stand
3 Edrich Stand
4 Compton Stand
5 match ground
6 nursery ground
7 future indoor

cricket school
8 future Test and County
Cricket Board offices
and shop
9 entrance
10 future arbours
11 future residential
development

The stand's open arcade
offers passers-by
tantalising glimpses
through the railings into
the ambulatory, which on
match days is alive with
members and spectators
moving to their seats
or hovering around the
bars, enjoying Lord's
secret life to the full.

Solid State Logic, 1986 – 1988

Solid State Logic, a company making sound-recording and broadcasting equipment, previously occupied a variety of buildings including an old garage, three standard factory sheds and a custom-designed building at Stonesfield, near Oxford, which looked a little like a parish church. In 1986 the company commissioned Hopkins to design a new building in the grounds of a converted country house at Begbroke, near Oxford. It was to accommodate manufacturing functions as well as offices.

Although the building was designed to be used essentially as a factory, it has none of the linear, indeterminate characteristics normally associated with that building type. It has two storeys and is perfectly square on plan, with a flat roof and a central top-lit atrium. The first floor overhangs the ground floor around the whole perimeter, shading the lower level. Circular fireproofed steel columns on a 7.2 metre grid support a concrete first-floor slab. On the upper floor the span is doubled and the columns support a steel space deck, partially concealed behind a perforated-metal suspended ceiling. External walls are all glass, except for metal louvres around plant rooms.

The original intention was to accommodate manufacturing functions on the ground floor and place offices above but the abstract nature of the plan, which allows partitions to be placed anywhere on an 1800mm grid, allows a high degree of flexibility of use. Despite this, the building gives an impression of solidity and permanence, partly because of its Palladian, square plan and partly because of the treatment of the first-floor slab. This has an exposed soffit, coffered with shallow domes to take circular glass light fittings, and is shot-blasted to enhance its stone-like quality. Horizontal services are housed within a 400mm high raised floor on top of the slab and at roof level in the space deck.

Although the external walls are all glass, this is an energy-saving building, naturally ventilated with some mechanical assistance, but not air-conditioned. Its compact plan minimises heat loss through the external envelope and heat gain is controlled by a variety of environmental filters. The glass is tinted grey and full-height sliding windows provide natural ventilation. On the first floor these open onto narrow metal balconies with handrails supported on subsidiary steel columns bracketed off the main structure. The main function of these subsidiary columns is to support external motorised venetian blinds, which are adjusted automatically. No blinds are required on the ground floor, which is shaded by the 1300mm first-floor overhang.

The four angled external staircases serve as fire escapes but they also tie the building into its mature garden setting. This is a high-quality, refined, almost monumental piece of architecture: a Miesian pavilion, rather than a High-Tech factory shed.

Location plan

Hopkins' building houses the manufacturing part of Solid State Logic's operation on the ground floor together with related functions such as design, and research and development on the floor above; a top-lit central atrium links these two levels.

Section through atrium
1 entrance
2 atrium
3 console assembly
4 component assembly
5 administration
6 research and development

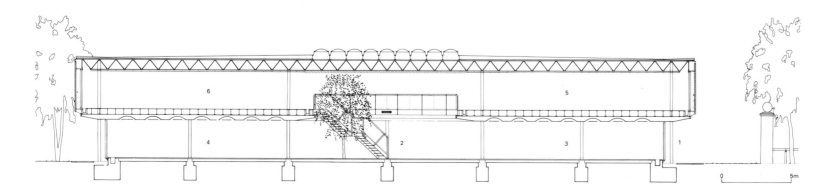

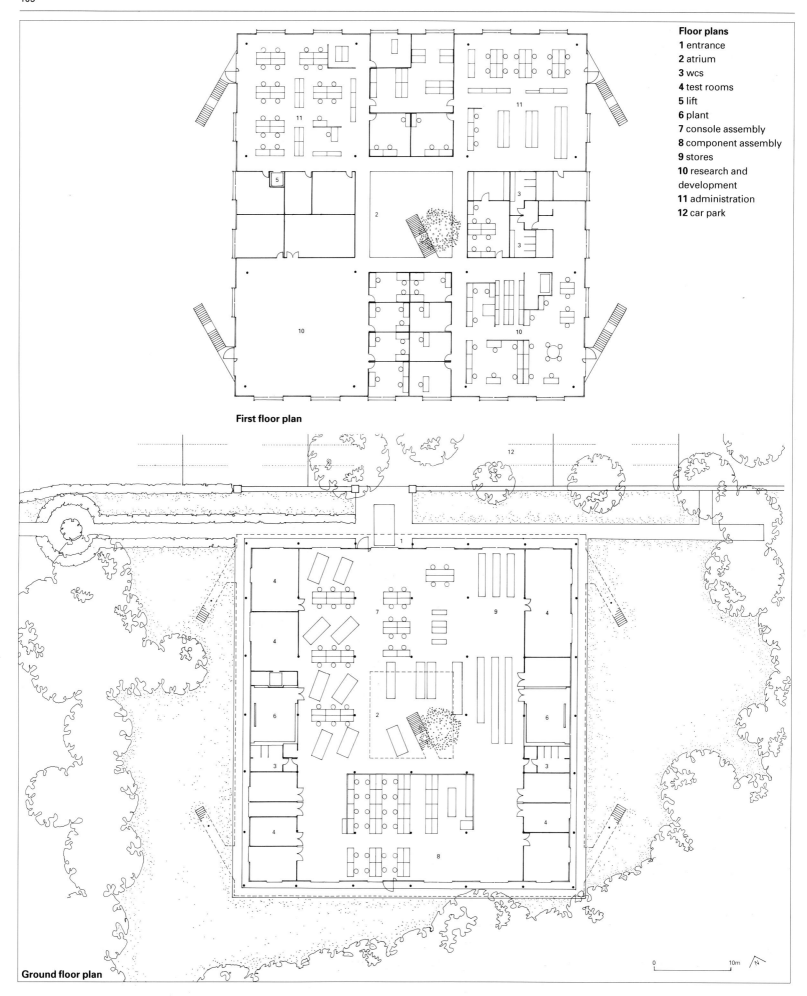

Floor plans
1 entrance
2 atrium
3 wcs
4 test rooms
5 lift
6 plant
7 console assembly
8 component assembly
9 stores
10 research and development
11 administration
12 car park

First floor plan

Ground floor plan

0   10m

Solid State Logic is a
highly transparent and
open building; its
windows can be slid back
in the summer, and the
full-height glazing makes
the wooded garden
setting very much part of
the internal environment
all year round.

David Mellor Cutlery Factory, 1988–1989

David Mellor is a cutler and one of the last surviving high-quality manufacturers in the Sheffield area. The setting of this small workshop, in the village of Hathersage on the edge of the Peak District, is rural but the site itself has an industrial past as it used to be the local gasworks. Planning permission for the building was granted largely because it reuses the old gasholder's foundations and leaves the landscape undisturbed; this accounts for its circular form.

An external wall of local stone, traditionally detailed but with precast concrete quoins and padstones, forms a drum supporting a shallow-pitched radial roof structure of lightweight steel trusses. These are tied together at the perimeter by adjustable tensile rods and at the centre by a sloping ring-truss around a conical, glazed lantern. The lantern itself is supported by a second radial structure like a bicycle wheel with an elongated spindle. The whole assembly is structurally rigid, so that it spans the entire space but exerts no lateral force on the supporting wall. Each truss is propped up off the concrete padstones on top of the wall, leaving a glazed slot around the whole building so that the shallow roof cone appears to float freely above the stone drum.

The roof covering is of traditionally detailed lead on a stepped deck made from prefabricated, stressed-skin, insulated plywood boxes, each tapered to conform to the radial pattern. These are fixed by means of steel hooks to tubular-steel purlins on top of the trusses. Boxes are used instead of a single-layer deck in order to provide the continuous, ventilated cavity above the insulation that is necessary to prevent condensation and possible corrosion of the lead. The roof has no gutter; rainwater falls from the eaves into a precast-concrete channel at ground level. Mellor supervised the construction himself and his own workforce made many of the components, including the plywood boxes and the precast-concrete quoins and padstones.

Inside the building, the functions that need to be enclosed – such as wcs, plant spaces and noisy machinery – are accommodated in two free standing rectangular boxes. Otherwise the space is open and loosely organised.

Despite its traditional appearance, this building is not a new building dressed up like an old one. As in all Hopkins' buildings, the design of every element conforms to a strict functional logic. The masonry drum, for example, is not merely a facing to a frame structure, but a true loadbearing wall. This fact, and the requirement for an open, column-free interior, dictated the design of the ingenious radial roof structure. All the components of this structure – tension rods, trusses and ring beams – are exposed and express their functions clearly. The result has the simplicity and power of the best 19th century industrial buildings – the sort that inspired the pioneers of the Modern Movement.

HATHERSAGE

B6001

from Sheffield

Location plan

Detail section through roof and wall

1 existing circular gasometer slab
2 cantilever reinforced-concrete slab
3 perimeter precast concrete drainage channel
4 loadbearing stone wall
5 insulating block inner skin

6 steel 'leaf-spring' bearing on precast concrete padstone
7 tubular-steel truss
8 lead-clad plywood box panel hooked over CHS purlin
9 ventilator
10 'bicycle wheel' compression strut
11 glazed conical rooflight

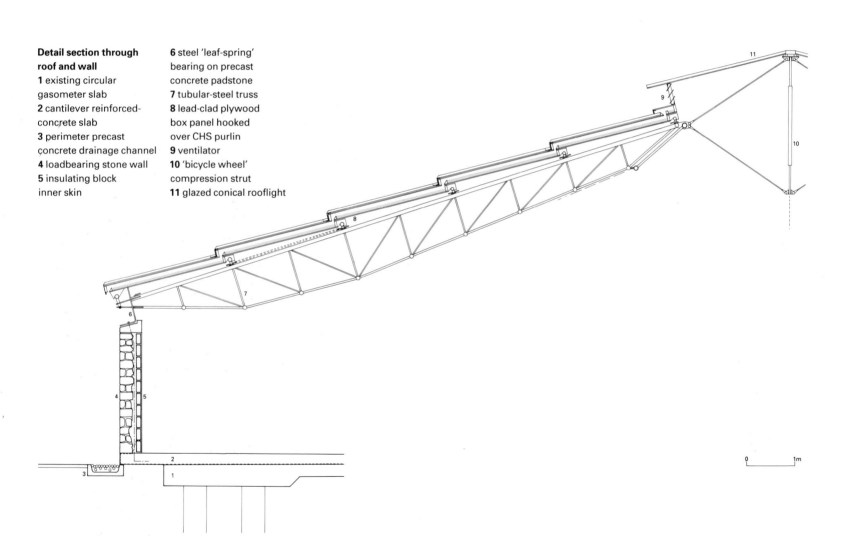

0   1m

Hopkins' building at
Hathersage is in part a
contextual response
to the surviving 19th-
century buildings on the
site, which have solid
stone walls and plated
iron roof trusses; but it is
also one stage in a
continuing investigation
into metal and masonry
construction.

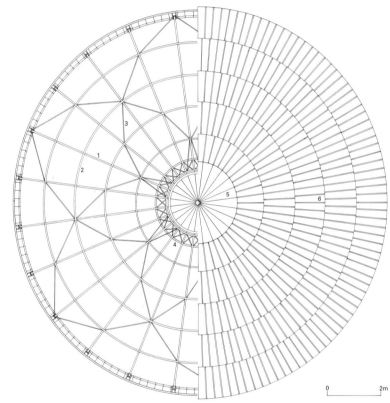

Roof plan
1 radial steel truss
2 circular steel purlins
3 cross bracing
4 conical ring truss
5 central glazed
rooflight
6 lead-clad
plywood panels

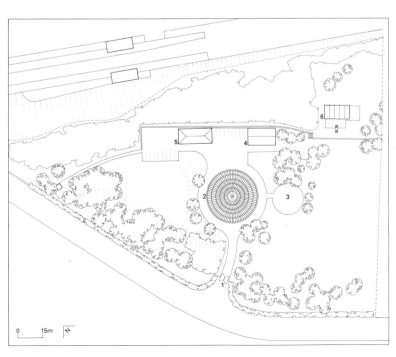

Site plan
1 entrance
2 cutlery factory
3 future expansion
4 Old Pump House office
5 factory shop
6 future private house

At Hathersage, Hopkins and David Mellor pioneered the working relationship that they continued at Shad Thames. Mellor took a keen interest in the development of the design and undertook to manufacture many of the buildings' components and to supervise its construction. His team put down the concrete floor slab over the old gasholder foundations, built the masonry walls and cast the concrete padstones, and made all 480 of the tapering plywood boxes that form the roof construction. He also fitted out the completed shell.

David Mellor Offices and Showroom, 1988 – 1991

This, the second Hopkins building for David Mellor, houses the cutlery manufacturer's London showroom as well as offices and an apartment. Like the Hathersage factory, its site has a 19th century industrial history, though here the setting is intensely urban – the old London dockside street known as Shad Thames. Mellor was not just the client, he was also a collaborator in the design and construction manager.

A simple six-storey glazed box, with its top floor set back to form roof terraces, is flanked by two service towers, one containing the main staircase and lift, the other containing plant rooms, wcs and a secondary staircase. This separation of 'served' and 'servant' spaces has enabled the main volume to be detailed in the simplest way possible. The building is naturally ventilated and the floor plates are small enough to allow heating by domestic-scale plant on each floor, which blows warm air across the space from one side. Suspended ceilings and raised floors, therefore, have been eliminated. The structural frame is concrete, which obviates the need for fireproofing. Round columns support flat slabs with exposed soffits and no downstand beams. Light fittings and conduits are cast into the slab, and power cables are housed in channels set into a cement floor screed. Full-height sliding windows are inserted between the columns on the front and back elevations, so that the true constructional nature of the building is apparent inside and out. In the flank walls steel-framed, lead-covered cladding panels take the place of sliding windows.

This degree of simplicity and refinement was not easy to achieve technically. Mellor and Hopkins went to great lengths to ensure a concrete finish that was precise and true, while preserving the moulded quality of the material. Plywood formwork was ordered to a special size and two types of joint were devised – a recessed joint formed by a specially developed aluminium extrusion and a secondary, projecting joint formed by chamferring the edges of the plywood panels.

The main staircase and lift tower display the same qualities of simplicity and solidity, though achieved by very different means. Here the distinction between structure and enclosing wall has disappeared altogether. Flanged steel panels are bolted together like the superstructure of a ship. The tower is unheated and has no insulation or lining.

On the top two, apartment, floors the austere design is lightened by terrace balustrades and balconies front and back. Each balcony is a separate steel component, with a gridded floor, slung off the main structure by diagonal tension rods. The concrete frame, however, remains the dominant element – a solid, handcrafted structure that represents the opposite of Hopkins' earlier industrialised 'kit-of-parts' approach. What has not changed, however, is the completely honest expression of construction and materials.

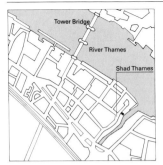

Location plan

Located in what was once the grim brick canyon of Shad Thames, David Mellor's London headquarters is very much a hand-crafted structure, and in that sense it can be seen as the descendant of the Victorian warehouses that once occupied the site.

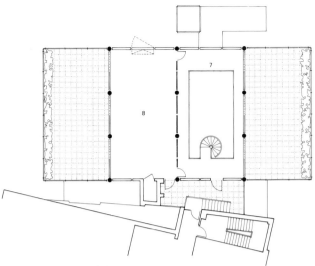

Apartment upper-level plan

Floor plans
1 showroom
2 upper level of showroom
3 hall
4 living
5 kitchen
6 bedroom
7 gallery
8 study

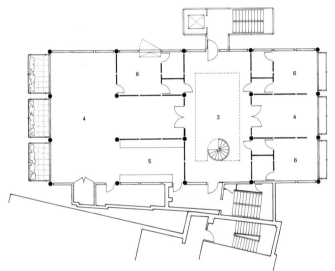

Apartment entrance-level plan

Above a ground-floor showroom, which enjoys spectacular river views, the building provides three floors of lettable office space and a duplex apartment, whose top storey is set back to form terraces on the river and street frontages.

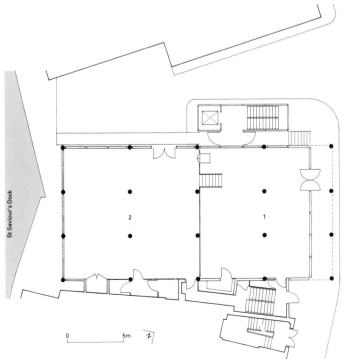

Ground floor plan

St Saviour's Dock

Shad Thames

0   5m

The Shad Thames
building is conceived as
appropriately 'utilitarian':
it is modest and well
suited to its task but is
beautifully made and, in
that sense, continues
a tradition of design and
manufacture that
Mellor has followed as
an industrial designer
and cutler.

Steel balustrading and
projecting balconies
define the building's top
two, apartment, floors
and relieve the
deliberate austerity of
the riverside and street
elevations.

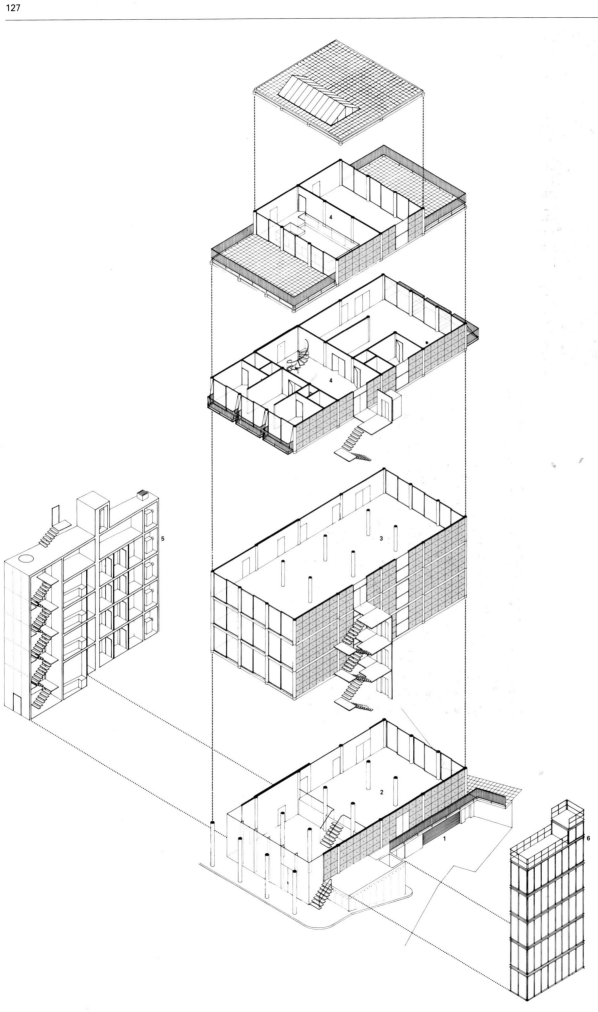

Exploded isometric view
1 car park
2 showroom
3 offices
4 apartment
5 services
6 stair and lift tower

Hopkins' habitual truth to materials has never been more consistently expressed than at Shad Thames: the concrete structure, metal-framed lift tower, lead-covered cladding panels and glazed elevations each contribute to the clarity of this statement.

The New Square development at Bedfont Lakes came about as the result of an agreement with the local authority: a large area of wasteland was reclaimed and converted into a country park in exchange for planning permission for offices suitable for multinational companies needing a base just a few minutes' drive from Heathrow Airport. There was a clear precedent for this kind of development at nearby Stockley Park, which has an informal, suburban layout, with pavilion-like buildings surrounded by landscaped car parks. At Bedfont Lakes, however, increased land costs dictated a higher density development with underground car parking. This suggested a more formal, urban solution.

Hopkins' masterplan takes the form of a single square, approximately the same size as Berkeley Square in the West End of London. Three-storey, air-conditioned office buildings, 18 metres deep, surround a triple-level, sunken car park. Hopkins was responsible for the three buildings at the northern end of the square, all designed for occupation by IBM, who were the co-developers of the project.

The remaining buildings were designed by other architects in accordance with the masterplan. Hopkins' buildings are firmly in the Miesian tradition, displaying all the abstract virtues of truth to materials, geometrical regularity and extreme refinement. The key element is an exposed steel frame, incorporating a new invention: a standard casting that connects columns and beams and cleverly accommodates the differences between the sizes of the columns at each level. The frames are infilled with identical glass and grey-painted aluminium panels, each equipped with a set of fixed external louvres.

In the largest of the three buildings, at the end of the square, the 18-metre deep plan is wrapped around a central atrium in which the steel frame is again exposed. This quasi-external space is roofed over by an almost flat, clear-glass membrane, suspended from a lattice-steel structure spanning the whole width of the space. Fabric sun shades are stretched between the trusses above the glass. In the middle of the three-storey space stands a steel and glass assemblage of bridges, lift shafts and a long, straight staircase. This divides the floor space into two zones, one for the restaurant, the other for a demonstration area to be used by IBM's marketing department. The surrounding floors are open to the atrium, though IBM has chosen to erect glazed partitions between the office space proper and the circulation gallery.

In each of the smaller, flanking blocks the full-height entrance hall is glazed from top to bottom on both sides and has an elegant spiral staircase.

Hopkins was also responsible for the detailed design of the car park. At ground level the layout takes the form of twin ellipses, surrounded by trees. The lower levels are lit by daylight filtering down through wells in the ellipses.

Location plan

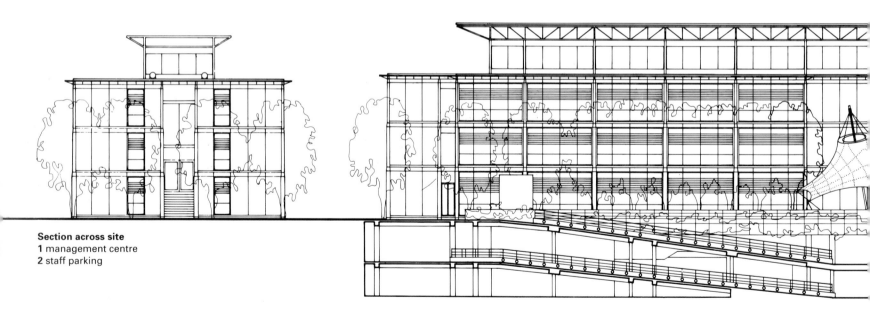

Section across site
1 management centre
2 staff parking

The Bedfont Lakes buildings enclose a formal garden square in which there are two elliptical car parks surrounded by trees. Below ground are two more car-parking levels, day-lit and ventilated by open wells.

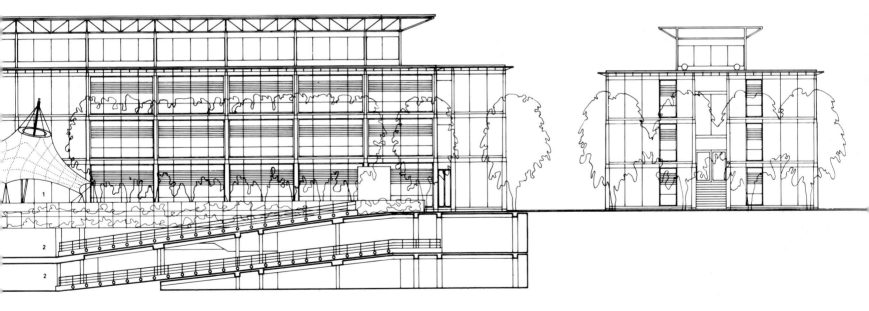

The central atrium in the largest of Hopkins' three office blocks is roofed by a taut, almost flat, glass skin suspended from a tubular-steel lattice structure that spans the full width of the space with no intermediate supports.

The underground car park
is the largest structure on
the site; its detailing is
as impressive as its scale,
with lighting and
mechanical plant well
integrated. From the
car park, one enters the
surrounding office
blocks via underground
passage ways.

Six

Five

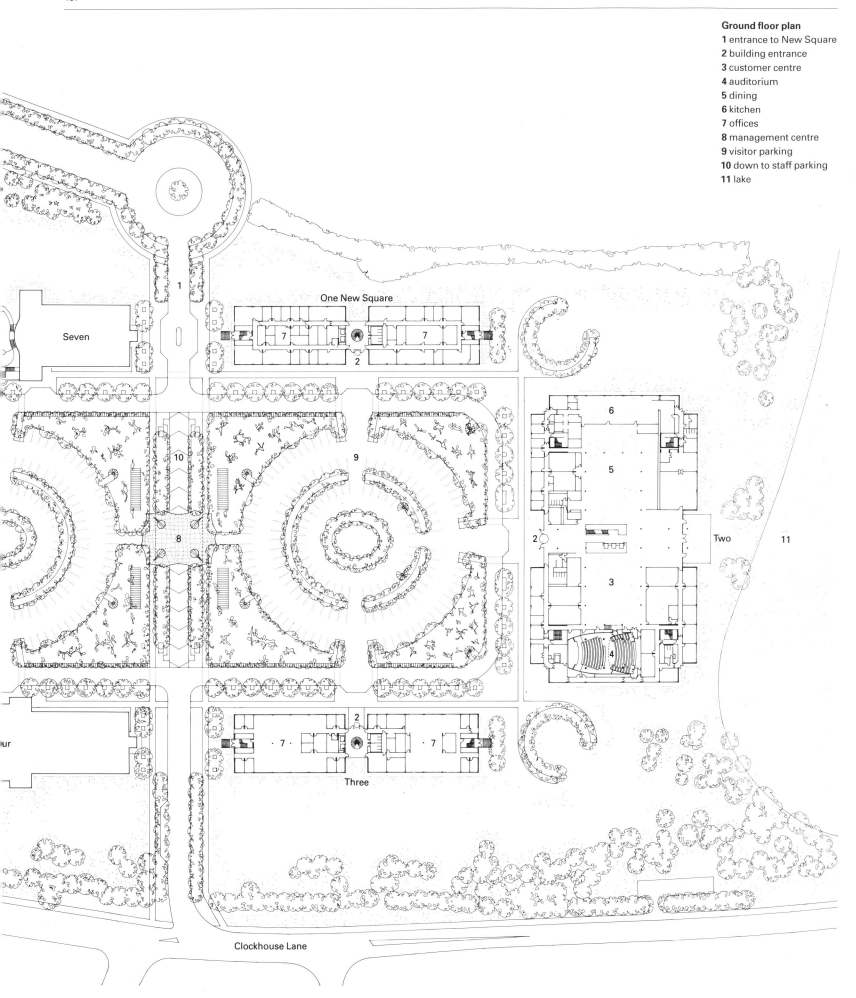

Ground floor plan
1 entrance to New Square
2 building entrance
3 customer centre
4 auditorium
5 dining
6 kitchen
7 offices
8 management centre
9 visitor parking
10 down to staff parking
11 lake

Seven

One New Square

Two

Three

Clockhouse Lane

The steel frame is
exposed both on the
facades and in the atrium;
a special nodal casting
connects columns and
beams, which tapers to
suit the diminishing
column dimensions from
one floor to the next.

Bedfont Lakes' formal
arrangement has its
origins in the dense urban
square, but here the
buildings are isolated
in the open landscape.
At the centre of the
scheme, a peaked tensile-
fabric canopy marks the
main reception and
the vehicular entrance to
the underground car park.

Bracken House, 1987 – 1992

In 1952 the chairman of the Financial Times, Brendan Bracken, commissioned Sir Albert Richardson to design a new building for the newspaper on an island site near St Paul's Cathedral in the heart of the City of London. The building was completed in 1959. Richardson's design, inspired by Guarino Guarini's Palazzo Carignano in Turin of 1679, placed two seven-storey office wings on either side of a printing works, screened by stone walls. The printing works was meant to correspond to the elliptical centre block in Guarini's palazzo but cost-cutting during construction forced Richardson to simplify its form to an octagon.

In 1987 the building was listed as being of historic value, but had also outlived its usefulness as a printing works; and the *Financial Times* had commissioned Nicholas Grimshaw to design a new building on the Isle of Dogs in London's docklands east of the City. The Obayashi Corporation of Japan bought Bracken House and commissioned Hopkins to convert it to an office building suitable for use by a financial institution, and in a way that would respect both Richardson's building as well as the sensitive urban site.

The two office wings are fine examples of Richardson's late, Classical style. Pink-red brickwork is the main material with bronze window frames, a base of Hollington stone and an attic storey sheathed in copper. In Hopkins' design, these wings are retained but the printing works is replaced by a new, deep-plan office block with a radial structure extending from a rectangular, central atrium. The curved outline of the block easily accommodates the different angles of the wings and the whole composition recalls Richardson's palazzo. A three-storey basement houses a large dealing room at the first level, with car parking and plant rooms below. The new facades are divided horizontally into three bands corresponding to the base, shaft and entablature of a Classical order.

The office wings are retained as complete buildings, not merely as facades, but their interiors have been rearranged to accommodate escape staircases, lavatories and service risers, as well as cellular offices. This leaves the floors of the main block completely open, interrupted only by the top-lit atrium with its central tower of four passenger lifts. A two-storey entrance hall on the east side of the building leads directly to the atrium. This is balanced by a service- and car-park entrance behind it.

In the new block, raised floors accommodate air-conditioning ducts as well as cabling. This allows the downstand beams of the main, reinforced-concrete structure to be exposed in the ceiling. The pattern of the structure therefore is clearly legible, with the beams radiating from the atrium to a ring of columns set back from the perimeter. Light fittings are recessed in areas of suspended ceiling between the beams.

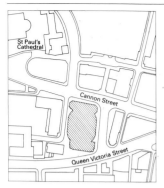

Location plan

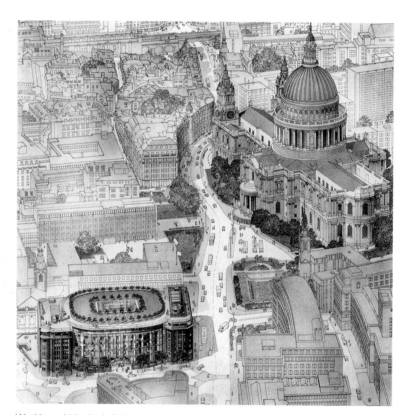

Working within the height
limitations set by St
Paul's Cathedral, Hopkins
inserted a new office core
between the retained
wings of Albert
Richardson's Bracken
House, redefining the
composition in
the process.

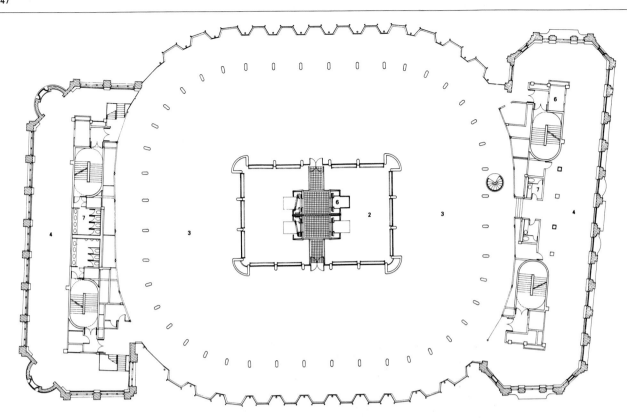

Typical upper floor plan

Floor plans
1 main entrance
2 atrium
3 new office area
4 retained office area
5 loading bay
6 lift
7 wcs

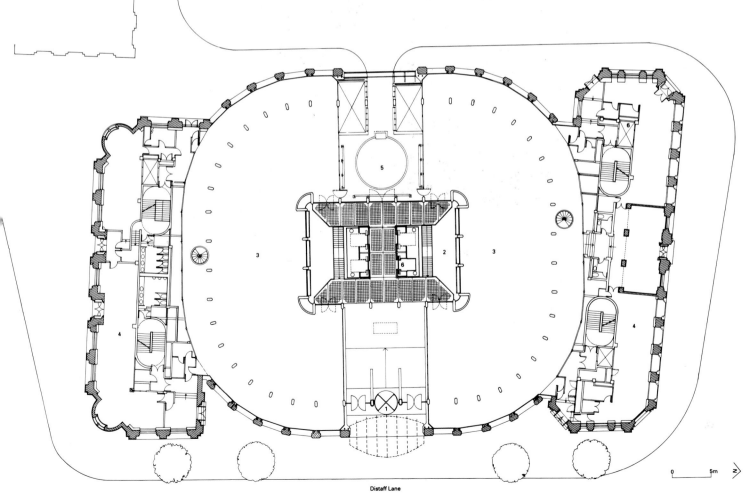

Distaff Lane

Ground floor plan

Hopkins' new facades use
materials found in the
retained sections from
the existing building:
Hollington sandstone,
bronze and glass; the
stone piers at ground
level provide a base for
the tri-armed bronze
castings that support the
facade glazing system.

The irregularity of
Bracken House's site
means that the
relationship between the
retained wings and
Hopkins' curving facade
is uneven. The junction
is handled discreetly,
with the irregularities
masked by deep recesses,
which maintain the
harmony of the whole.

**Section through atrium
and lift shaft**
1 main entrance
2 atrium
3 new office area
4 dealer floor
5 loading bay
6 lift
7 car park
8 service area

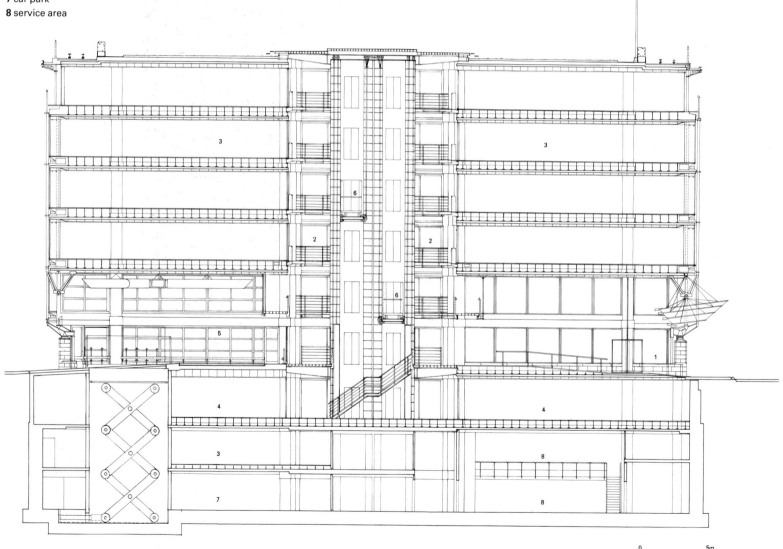

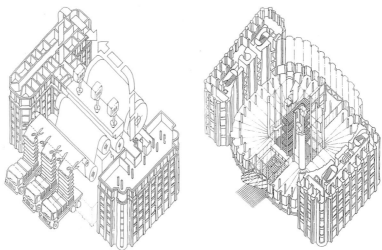

Witty sketches, taken from the Hopkins office's initial report to the client, show Bracken House's conceptual transformation from printing plant to commercial palazzo.

Hopkins' new central structure at Bracken House is focused on a rectangular atrium, which contains the building's lifts that connect, via glass-decked walkways, to the office floors. The lift shafts were not allowed to project above the roofline because of the height restrictions imposed by St Paul's; consequently, the motor rooms are located in the basement, allowing the atrium's flat glass roof to span clearly above the tops of the shafts.

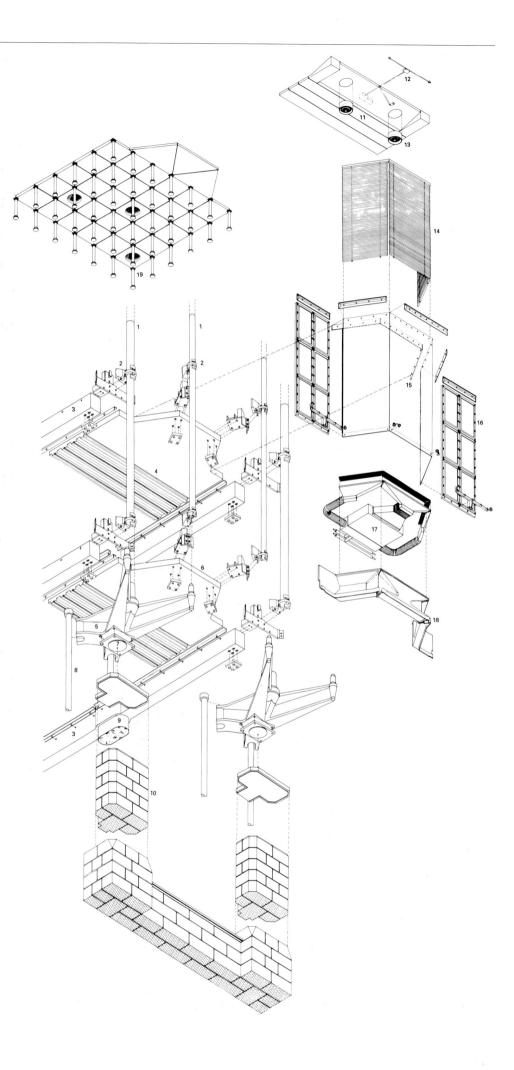

**Exploded isometric
view of bay components**
1 gunmetal column
2 column connector
3 precast concrete beam
4 steel permanent
formwork
5 cast gunmetal
base bracket
6 fairfaced concrete
bay slab
7 stainless steel rocker
bearing
8 stainless steel
tension rod
9 in-situ concrete column
10 loadbearing Hollington
stone pier
11 perforated steel
ceiling planks
12 light-sensitive
blind control
13 perimeter light fittings
14 venetian blinds
15 toughened double-
glazed suspended
bay window
16 bronze smoke vents
17 fan cowl unit
18 pressed bronze
coiling
19 raised computer floor

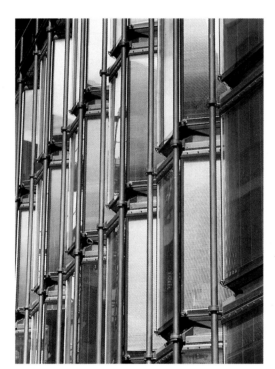

The architectural character of Bracken House's office glazing results directly from the way that materials are chosen and components are assembled. At first-floor level, bearing on the stone piers, are bronze brackets that cantilever out to support the columns on the face of the bay windows; these brackets are tied down at the back by stainless steel rods. The bronze columns rise through four floors and are bracketed to support the leading edge of the floor beams; the horizontal plates and bolts of the brackets are expressed on the ceilings inside. The frameless glazing is suspended from bronze clamps at each floor level; the double-glazed units are secured to one another by planar clamps. There are no openings in the major glazing sections; opening lights for smoke ventilation are located between the bays.

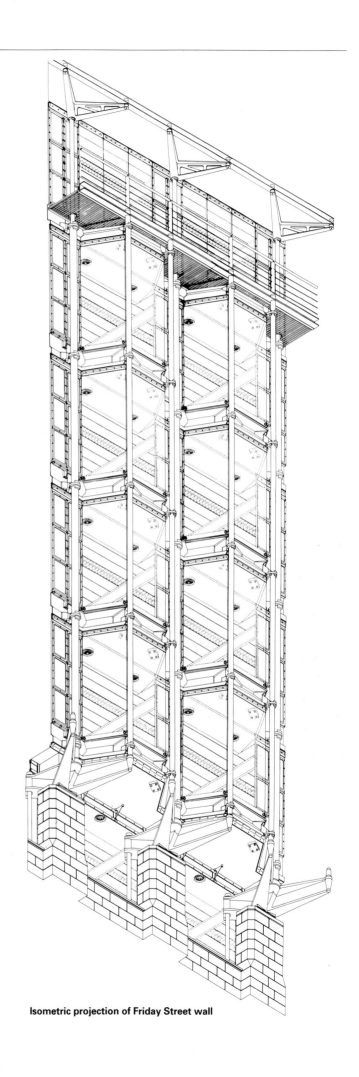

Isometric projection of Friday Street wall

An English Sensibility: the making of an architectural technology

Patrick Hodgkinson

Bracken House, City of
London, 1992.

Architecture and language

Perhaps not surprisingly in a world quick with labels, Michael Hopkins' work has been considered as being of the High-Tech school – his hand, after all, helped with some of Norman Foster's formative buildings – yet his own recent projects less and less wear the imagery of that *genre*. We can look for attempts to make a syntax for a language of architecture, but in that particular quarter leading figures have, to more open viewpoints, too often become technocrats of restricted imagination, their buildings lining up in stylised uniforms like bellboys handy with parrot-speak. Their language for the different purposes of buildings is therefore limited compared with that of an architect of the stature of the late James Stirling, for example, whatever reservations we might have with his *parti*. Against all that, it is better to understand where Hopkins links with a modern inheritance and then to consider whether he is interpreting it into a richer, more useful language.

The main dialect that arose from Modernism's 'heroic period' abstracted a Classical past, its minimalism decried by free-thinkers of the time. And wisely, for it produced architecture that was to disenchant society: the disenchantment perhaps of Aldous Huxley's character, Gumbril, in *Antic Hay*, who raged against the 'vile and discordant' buildings people seemed not to notice as they would a discordant brass band. Gumbril's explanation: 'The fact is that architecture is a more difficult and intellectual art than music. Music – that's just a faculty you're born with, as you might be born with a snub nose. But the sense of plastic beauty – though that's, of course, an inborn faculty – is something that has to be developed and intellectually ripened. It's an affair of the mind; experience and thought have to draw it out'. Nothing said, though, of those touchstones of the past, which most people need when approaching the future, but I shall return to memory later.

Until the dawn of modern science the Latin *ars* described construction craft in architecture, while *scientia* referred to geometry and theories of proportion. For us, 'technology' covers no more than construction science. As with the Latin definition, whereas the earlier Greek *teknologia* (where *tekne* = art) meant 'systematic treatment' of all constituents of an artefact together, the 19th century removed art from science so that science, unlike alchemy of old, is just a number of separate laws for analysing the material aspects of matter. We are therefore left without guidelines for satisfying that essential kingdom of the mind and eye – aesthetics. We are loosely aware that beauty in most man-made things is inseparable from the know-how of science or craft, yet it is not enough to leave the question to Huxley's aesthete. Nor should we tolerate buildings which, for the sake of imposed image, continue to borrow technologies from other spheres. Rather, we need to develop specific architectural technologies where creative thought is part of a scientific equation. It is precisely here that the Hopkins thrust is signal and why his revived Bracken House in London deserves especial attention. The building somehow goes beyond that old formula, architecture = science + art.

The English Free School, partly through Herman Muthesius' ministrations and his book, *Das Englische Haus*, had wide influence in Germany after the turn of this century because its buildings and furniture were seen as a native, craft culture that formed a basis for design. With that strong background at home, and it continued through the 1930s, it is clear why England was slow to adopt the Continental 'white box' aesthetic and why architects like William Lethaby, C R Mackintosh and C F A Voysey, who all witnessed its arrival here, abhorred the thought that this might have sprung from their own work. The International Style aesthetic arose from an earlier parting of the ways and was concerned with allusion through the imposed images of machines. The English Free School had concentrated on the reality of the traditionally known, which is touchable, immediate.

Within Continental Europe around 1925 there were two streams of Modernism: architects who fed from the Classical tradition and those who saw formal artifice as authoritarian and therefore opposed to a natural freedom of spirit. They looked instead for a reality hand-in-hand with forward-thinking philosophy. While a young Walter Gropius or Mies van der Rohe had wavered earlier, the first group set up CIAM (Congrès

William Lethaby:
English Free School
Church, Brockhampton,
Hereford, 1901.

Internationaux de l'Architecture Moderne) and became its leaders, while those surrounding Hugo Häring in Berlin were largely ignored, especially by Siegfried Giedion's *Space, Time and Architecture*, first published in 1941.

Erich Mendelsohn, whose Einstein Tower of 1921 was the first permanent manifestation of Modernism in Europe, was the most important architect of this second group at the time. He went on to build his hat factory at Luckenwald, houses and office blocks in Berlin and his various department stores for the Schocken empire, and with these achievements so early it can only have been racial prejudice that barred Mendelsohn from building for the Weissenhoff Siedlung exhibition at Stuttgart in 1927 and then from CIAM the next year – ironic when those against him also claimed to be working towards freedom.

It was Mendelsohn's Schocken stores that inspired the young William Crabtree, for instance, in his designs for the Peter Jones department store in Sloane Square, London, in 1934: a building that showed a more constructive attitude to townmaking than the 'object' projects that followed CIAM thinking. Mendelsohn's beliefs sprang directly from Futurism (not Expressionism, as some historians hold), rather than the Cubist leanings of the CIAM group. His concern, like Häring's, was to do with life as it

Above, Erich Mendelsohn: Schocken Store, Stuttgart, 1927. Right, William Crabtree with Slater, Mowberly and Reilly: Peter Jones store, Chelsea, London, 1938.

is and the distinct purposes for which buildings are made. Functionalism has since been decried, but if we forget *purpose* as the prime instigator of architecture, both as space and for the shape of building elements, we quickly confuse the discipline with fine art. We may say that the Functionalism of Mendelsohn or Häring – and there were others like Alvar Aalto, Dominikus Böhm and Hans Scharoun who subscribed to equivalent beliefs – concerned itself not simply with an accommodation brief but with human use in its deepest, emotional sense.

If Post-Modernism is little more than paraphrase it is because it has nothing fresh to say. As such it may be the only route left to those who cast reality aside, preferring instead to rely on artifice. Since, apart from Vienna, Hopkins relates to those earlier, ignored figures rather than the formalist CIAM camp, comparisons between Bracken House and contemporary examples of Post-Modernism are apt. Beyond that, we might say Hopkins' direct concerns are with human purpose and the meaning of building elements in terms of their functions, but there is also a deep appreciation of the psyche's need for memory in order that we are placed in time: time meaning not just today but in relation to our pasts and possible futures, often through the use of mass and materials we associate with longevity. Such relationships also reflect the needs within us of permanence and transience and also of closed and open space together. For Hopkins the 'functional' resolution is not an end in itself, but it is often the means by which understandable form can be given to a building's parts, accepting that there are other means of mnemonic reference than appealing to the Orders.

Instancing a few of Michael Hopkins and Partners' buildings, the Greene King Draught Beer Cellars at Bury St Edmunds and the Schlumberger Cambridge Research Centre are both located on sites without former human associations. Functional answers for the processes to be housed, which referred only to the present, were appropriate. At the Mound Stand at Lord's Cricket Ground in London and the buildings for David Mellor at Hathersage and in London Docklands there were different, centuries-old associations with human life and in each case, as with Bracken House itself, means were found to relate to those

Top left, Erich Mendelsohn: Einstein Tower, Potsdam, 1921. Top right, Dominikus Böhm: Friedlingsdorf church, Cologne, 1927. Bottom, Hugo Häring: Garkau Farm, near Lübeck, 1925.

Above left, Georges Chedanne: *Parisien Libéré* building, Paris, 1904. Above right, C R Mackintosh: Glasgow School of Art, 1908.

backgrounds. Instead of more fashionable steel, the Offices and Showroom for David Mellor at Shad Thames, for example, uses a concrete frame for the main bulk with steel only enclosing the flanking escape staircases. As at Bracken House, however, advanced industrial techniques have produced a material of mass of impeccable accuracy and finish.

At Glyndebourne, the new opera house will be built in brick and lead, again to associate us with the extensiveness of time and the layers of history within our comprehension of this place. I am concerned here with idea: whatever Hopkins' inner predilections about historic association, the fundamental factor is that memory and time are legitimate aspects of an architectural technology that pure engineering technologies do not encompass, just as rammed earth – and not just for developing countries – may be seen as technologically advanced in certain circumstances today because it is economical and full of architectonic potential at the same time. The High-Tech we know has generally used 'advanced' engineering technologies only, without acknowledging their full architectural consequences and often without recourse to economy of means.

In these respects we can appreciate Mackintosh's Glasgow School of Art as not only using an appropriate building system for its time, but still serving its purpose, perhaps more honourably than more 'modern' buildings, while Gillespie, Kidd and Coia's church at East Kilbride of 1964 used richly complex brickwork detailing, which fastened the building to the memory of its congregation. At Bracken House the gunmetal detailing – an essential part of the technological concept – is an equivalent, resulting from a craftsman's fascination with the projecting oriels and steel facade elements of Georges Chedanne's 1904 *Parisien Libéré* building on rue Réaumur in Paris.

Gothic phoenix, Classic support? Bracken House revived

'Oh! And make it pink, Richardson, like my newspaper. See you at Topping Out', might well have been Brendan Bracken's farewell to Albert Richardson (knighted with this final work, Bracken already a peer) after choosing an architect who would

Gillespie, Kidd and Coia: St Brides, East Kilbride, 1964.

make his *Financial Times* headquarters' building look as though it had always been there.

Bracken House opened in 1959, the ceremony distracted by a bunch of Royal College of Art Anti-Ugly students laying their coffin of Modern architecture at its threshold. However backward-looking, the building had a certain authority not possessed by its fellows arising on bomb sites surrounding St Paul's Cathedral. Two decades earlier in modern spirit, though, Peter Jones in Sloane Square had shown its masterful urban assurance. But remember, London's West End was just considered an evening playground, a woman's world, by any hardnosed, City man of business. There is also, hereabouts, sacred English ritual: black shoes for town, brown for country; be sure to get the fundamentals of life right. *Everything in its place*. A while ago an important someone saw nothing wrong with Mies' Mansion House tower so long as it was put in Luton.

All this is serious and it persists. Coming, as it were, to Rome, Obayashi Europe BV, the freeholder and client for the revived Bracken House, sensibly did as the Romans; but somewhat better. Their choice of architect in Michael Hopkins has produced a building of rare excellence and with a Savile Row pedigree. The bare interior concrete was hand-pummiced lovingly to give it the svelte look of English grey flannel and the intervention, inside and out, speaks aristocratically through the style of its handworked seams. That's the new part, the phoenix. Richardson's remaining but refurbished 'bookends' are another question. Together, old and new expose the arbitrariness of certain attitudes to heritage we need to question. Within these constraints, nevertheless, Hopkins and his team have developed a wholesome direction for British architecture. It puts to shame the conversations that led to the Sainsbury Wing of the National Gallery in London, for example.

That unsavoury dialogue sprang from the Janus factor of Victorian England, which still lurks. While engineers were applauded for their progressive constructions, *amour propre* seldom permitted architecture to follow. By 1860 when Isambard Kingdom Brunel, Robert Stevenson and John Locke had been honourably buried, almost together, the tempered

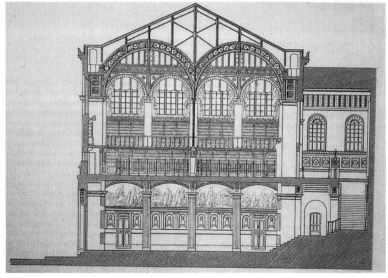

Right, Deane &
Woodward: Oxford
University Museum, 1860.
Far right, Henri Labrouste:
Bibliothèque Sainte-
Geneviève, Paris, 1850.

outlook of the South took precedence over the industrial North. Cast iron had been invented in England and was fine for bridges, train sheds and satanic mills, but not openly for the mother art. *Everything in its place*, of course. In Paris, Henri Labrouste's Bibliothèque Sainte-Geneviève of 1850 had displayed its cast-iron construction and many French architects followed. In England, apart from the Crystal Palace, which was just considered a shed even by Joseph Paxton, the few contemporary examples were undistinguished: Robert Smirke's British Museum reading room, where the innovative iron was hidden; Deane and Woodward's Oxford University Museum, its iron decorated to John Ruskin's command in the Gothick. A late exception was Peter Ellis' Oriel Chambers in Liverpool of 1865. At the same time Labrouste was already building his splendid Bibliothèque Nationale in Paris (completed in 1868) with its cast iron, top-lit reading room and remarkable cast and wrought iron bookstack, also lit from above. To the 'cultured' English, the French always had a vulgar streak.

Richardson's inspiration for his pile had been Guarino Guarini's Palazzo Carignano in Turin; roughly contemporary with St Paul's, but not at all Wren's straight-bat Baroque – far more sensuous. Turin was then only a provincial, commercial centre and these factors make it a strange choice. The original Bracken House plan followed the palazzo's in wayward spirit but the main entrance was placed on the wrong axis, misunderstanding the logic of Guarini's Classical grammar. Such an error would not have troubled a mind that considered a rendition of the curvilinear example to be appropriate in the 1950s but the eccentric Richardson, from his walled, Georgian seat in Bedfordshire or behind the wheel of his dear old Rolls Royce, dabbled in eclecticism.

As pastiche Sir Albert's Bracken House was fair. Materials that go together with metropolitan panache and mature with age were as carefully chosen as the external detailing was handled but, progressively, it was at least a century late. The concrete frame was clad in stone and brick, with bronze and cast iron for tall window assemblies and penthouses (bronze was the intention throughout but cost forced these elements of

the south wing to be in painted cast iron), could have been built in 1850. We had the means then, but not the will. A revival from a Baroque source would have been odd but not so strange a century earlier. The stylistic supporters of Richardson's fandango underline its formal urban ordering: base, middle, cornice and penthouse, yet Crabtree's Peter Jones had handled all of these with real subtlety. Newspaper offices need no more monumentality than a good quality department store; the two are similar in kind.

The old Bracken House was an 'H' in plan, the two wings housing offices and the link, the printing hall. Pearsons, the parent company of the *Financial Times*, first held a limited competition, which Hopkins won with a scheme replacing the whole building. It was 1987, just before the 30-year listing rule was adopted and another competitor, forseeing this, proposed retaining the wings but replacing the link. The old building had been acquired by Obayashi who retained Hopkins to build his winning proposal. Abracadabra! The whole building was suddenly listed and Hopkins had to redesign his first scheme to respect the checkmate. Between those bookends, therefore, he considerably increased the accommodation, within the height limitations for St Paul's, by inserting a new 'doughnut' of regular floors with a central, roof-lit atrium. The clarity of this

Right, Peter Ellis: Oriel Chambers, Liverpool, 1865.
Far right, Henri Labrouste: Bibliothèque Nationale reading room, Paris, 1868.

arrangement persuaded English Heritage and the City's planners to allow major alterations to the listed building. Game to Obayashi!

Hopkins' arrival at his new concept, illustrated by an early sketch plan, was, in a sense, fortuitous. He took Guarini's definitive plan for the central, linking block of the palazzo and doubled it about its cross axis, its symmetrical arcs intruding into the middle of Richardson's non-aligned wings. Guarini's plan had isolated his curvilinear geometry from his orthogonal wings as Classicism would, but the two intersecting ovals thus formed enabled the existing bookends to pivot in a manner no orthogonal insertion would have allowed. This concept re-established the entrance in its rightful place and the doubling of the one-way symmetrical plan, maximising floorspace, gave Hopkins' service bay an equivalent importance to the main entrance, presenting to Distaff Lane at the back an identical elevation to that of the new front onto Friday Street, save for its incisive, ice-glass tongue.

This idea – 'doughnut' within bookends – is the 'Classic support' of my subtitle. Returning to the concept sketch and a view of Guarini's main facade, although it may seem strange that lines have been drawn across the tips of the intersecting

Guarino Guarini:
Palazzo Carignano,
Turin, 1679.

ovals and that the third oval, the atrium, has become a rectangle thus tempering a series of potentially voluptuous forms, the difficult job of making any new building fit between and successfully bring the bookends together has been achieved with considerable skill. The concept is of organic origin and relates to other points I will make later about this Gothic phoenix.

The central, double-height entrance under a sprightly truss – its brittle glass canopy sprinkled with pinpoints of light – leads directly onto the glass floor of the atrium with stairways and daylight reaching down to the dealing room below. Freestanding steel lift shafts connected by daylight-filtering, glass-floored bridges at the upper levels, are placed centrally. This tall, hard space, surrounded by opening windows and the life these will engender with people in the glass lifts and on the bridges, has the friendly character of some once open-air yard, removed from the noise of the City outside. Its spirit is today's but it relates to the family of that older, softer world Norman Foster opened up under his Sackler Gallery at the Royal Academy in London, a human world of light, shadows, reflections – and intrigue. Like those open, *Hôtel Paradiso* lift cages, which used to travel up the wells of spiralling staircases in Paris, climbers and passengers throwing brickbats and bouquets at each other, the atrium expects life's humorous drama, not the stuffed shirts for whom Richardson had catered.

Where they are clear of the voids over entrance and service bay the four upper floors of the doughnut are each complete entities. At the atrium's corners are segmental, structural concrete shafts containing ducts, their heads bent outwards like back-stretched hands to accept the radiating beams supported at their outward ends by a peristyle of columns. This is inset from the oriented glass walls and the disturbed fabric of the bookends. It defines the general office areas. The shaping of the segmental shafts away from expected engineering forms but, with an eye to nature, is genius. While I have noted that the initial concept sketch first suggests a more curvilinear arrangement, these open floors are extremely satisfying. The peristyle announces 'room' but the atrium's shafts and movement prevent you seeing it all at once. Like a Gothic cathedral, the whole is revealed only by moving around it, yet the flow of the peristyle expects the entire space. A more fluid plan might well have compromised reasonable working layouts.

The heroic moment is in the new facades and the delicacy of their construction. Some bits of the bookends have necessarily been invented to form adequate couplings. Outside, they provide a sparkling female foil to Richardson's macho wings; within, the faceted oriels become aedicules surrounding the greater spaces, sometimes used for enclosed rooms, sometimes not. Intimacy dwells here. These wholly delightful constructions, which carry their own weight to the ground, pleated and like the massed tutus of a *corps de ballet*, join with the bookends as a flying Fonteyn might have been caught – only hands touching – by a Nureyev, with more than a touch of class. The clasp is made to seem inevitable.

The slender columns and tougher support brackets are cast gunmetal, which is also used in sheet form for spandrels and blind ventilators, with bronze for the frames to which sheets of double glazing are applied. They are substantially the same materials Richardson used, but technology and perhaps a look at the Gothick Oriel Chambers – far heavier – provides a grace that is breathtaking. I always considered the sinuous curtain wall of Peter Jones had never been bettered until the arrival of Foster's sleek sheath for Willis Faber & Dumas at Ipswich of 1975 (to which Hopkins himself contributed). But however technologically advanced, the predominant architecture represented in that curtain is the surrounding facades it mirrors. At Bracken House the oriel assemblies, which also carry the floorslab edges, bear down through the three-fingered brackets onto stone pillars that describe a base to the building; fragments, perhaps, of Richardson's solid base. This is the crux of Hopkins' architectural technology.

An ideological advance upon the Willis Faber & Dumas building, this constructional concept recalls those everlastingly wonderful stone and glass Gothic walls, as at King's Chapel, Cambridge, with their filigreed layering where buttress, pilaster,

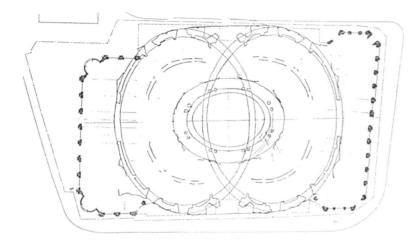

Top, Bracken House, City of London, 1992: concept sketch.
Bottom, Sir Albert Richardson: Bracken House, City of London, 1959.
Right, Bracken House, City of London, 1992.

mullion are somehow fused with the liquidity of glass, even the diaper lead cames providing their intricate part in the complexity. The architectural fecundity presiding at Bracken House (Hopkins cites Robert Smythson's Hardwick Hall as inspiration) is different, though, because the structure is metal and the glass, large panels of plate appropriate for offices.

My allusions to Gothic thinking in terms of space and layering are both dangerous and interesting. In neither case am I attempting to pigeonhole Hopkins, least of all as a revivalist. This is just good architecture, which draws new life, a new enlightenment, from an appropriately interpreted past. The danger lies in the fact that the cause and purpose of Gothic, rather than rationalising construction as Classical architecture had done – many Gothic structures can appear illogical in themselves – was to implant theosophical theories in the medieval mind. That was the misunderstanding of Augustus Pugin: there were no new summas to describe visually and by 1836, the date of his *Contrasts*, many people could read, write and think objectively and we should not fall into an equivalent trap. The interest is that the Modernism most of us accept, despite Frank Lloyd Wright and a few others to whom I have referred, spiked its crampon somewhere in the Classical cycle. That may have been natural in the 1920s and the persuaders were persuasive. But this was not the case with Futurism or Expressionism, movements that tried to leap clear of Classical authority to a new freedom of the mind, which is not dissimilar to the idea of aspiration of the soul expressed so evidently in Gothic. The fact is, though, that to achieve his ends Hopkins uses functional purpose to display an *idea* of the construction, accepting the formal and organic as partners as, for example, did the builders of Chartres, then Francesco Borromini and Guarini and more recently Antoni Gaudí, Alvar Aalto and the late Giovanni Michelucci.

The 'tech' at Bracken House is low. The general notion of High-Tech has been to push technology to its limits as if buildings were but machines. They are generally not. This thrust had its uses but it too quickly became an end in itself. Hopkins countered this narrow thinking by extending an

Foster Associates: Willis Faber Dumas, Ipswich, 1975.

existing arched masonry wall at his Mound Stand for Lord's Cricket Ground in London and by encircling his Hathersage roundhouse factory with a stone wall topped by a traditional lead roof. At Bracken House the mass of the stone piers roots the doughnut to the ground making the glass tutus seem all the more diaphanous. Inside, an equivalent attachment to earth is felt in the atrium's shafts, the peristyle of columns and the exposed downstand beams of the slabs, all giving a feeling of flowing permanence against the lighter metal components. It was Mackintosh who suspected that materials such as iron and glass 'will never worthily take the place of stone because of this defect, the want of mass', and many run-of-the-mill, all-lightweight buildings suggest he was right. They are but ephemera. Finding an interior finish for concrete that is acceptable is an equally important breakthrough, saving us now from excusing the material with art nonsense. In these respects and the futures his orielled walls provoke, Hopkins emerges from his *côterie* as a sage, perhaps also as a romantic.

Resplendent and bright in high summer, here is an unforbidding, truly City building, which glitters in rain and will enlighten the disgruntlement of winter. I am reminded of sophisticated ankles and the crack of high black heels on hard pavements. Oysters and Chablis at Sweetings, please, and don't forget the Tabasco. The elevating *zeitgeist* makes the literary English architecture of the Enlightenment itself – let alone its plastic pastiche today – look like a tired, drawing-room comedy still playing in the provinces.

Aside from the Pop Art of the 1960s – a momentary thing – it seems strange that Robert Venturi went to Las Vegas to find his complexity and contradiction when a deeper meaning with their uses can be found in a past of distinction, such as the Gothic I have evidenced. In 1851 Paxton's Crystal Palace, a realisation of architecture within a progressive, industrial idea, housed exhibits of excruciating taste accepted by a bourgeoisie who only saw the building itself as engineering. Now, with the soot out of industry but within an exhausted, popular theme of 'art gallery', the same theorist reflects only the *zeitgeist* of those Victorian exhibits for the architecture of his Sainsbury Wing at

Bracken House, City of London, 1992.

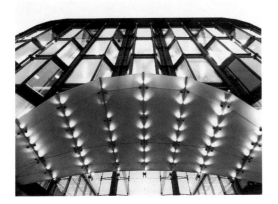

the National Gallery, while Hopkins, clear of an Art Nouveau overlay of nature, has developed the genre of Paxton's building into an architecture fully conscious of Viollet-le-Duc and life today. Can the justifiers of the former *reasonably* continue? Together with the anomalies of listing, Hopkins' stance may be read as a considered critique of the values these people hold.

In order to make development sense of retaining the Richardson wings with the servicing now expected in a building of this type – except for the original, now embalmed, entrance hall with its astrological clock, Winston Churchill's face representing the sun – the old interiors have been largely swept away. The original fenestration is not very suitable for today's working arrangements and the accommodation provided is second rate compared to the doughnut. Hopkins has done his best but the real wealth is in the books, not in their supports. We must deeply question whether or not we should preserve facades that are just pastiche, albeit done with dash. A whole new building of excellence on a site such as this might well have convinced the faint-hearted for other areas of sensitivity. It is one thing to keep a whole cake but quite another to hang on to the icing which was only there to preserve it. In this case the finishing coat slipped into the wrong century. The listing

Robert Smythson:
Hardwick Hall,
Derbyshire, 1593.

process is often used to prevent bad buildings replacing good. The policy here has clipped the wings of an architect of rare ability whose original competition entry could well have faced up to the St Paul's we know just as, it seems, he will rise to the occasion of the Palace of Westminster in Bridge Street.

Above the restaurant floor, which formally answers Richardson's penthouses in terms of neo-Classical facade grammar, a splendid, lawned roof garden overlooked by St Paul's is yet to be completed. The hiccup seems foolish because the garden was intended, as within the City of old, to provide a little acre of sanctity above this Mauritania of electronics and efficiency. Perhaps the incessant work ethic in the Japanese character cannot digest such a need? Nevertheless, the atmosphere of the building provides the tenants, the Industrial Bank of Japan, with a civilised reasoning for their corporate image, notwithstanding the amount of energy consumed. It is precisely here, though, that the already weak conservation argument is not tolerable. Considerations such as this are not easy in the City's square mile, but if Brendan Bracken told his architect to think pink, Yoshiro Obayashi – without the gag of a sudden listing – might well have supported his architect to lean green. A whole new building would have stood a chance of achieving something that blinkered eyes failed to acknowledge. The completion of the roof garden would give back an essential contributor to the wholesomeness of Hopkins' concept.

If *amour propre* is to become progressive, and our mandarins of taste, including public figures, are perceptive, they will realise that behind the intricate glass wall to Friday Street is a world of elegant ideas, perhaps as important to a future British architecture as the Hong Kong and Shanghai Bank was internationally eight years ago. In this sense, and because it delights in the live aspects of our national culture and includes them within its technological language, Hopkins' revived Bracken House – albeit a forced compromise at first appearing as unfortunate as St Paul's itself – may be seen as a milestone in as many years hence.

It is important that here is an architecture whose language is uncluttered by some lost meaning of Classicism or that of any equivalent historic cycle or style. It is therefore understandable to the sensibilities we use to evaluate other contemporary art forms. I have referred to the unsavoury Janus factor of Victorian England still lurking in terms of Post-Modernism and it is this comparison we must make to realise why Hopkins has adopted the stance that Bracken House displays so eloquently. *Everything in its place* should be seen in terms of the distance society has travelled since Brendan Bracken and Albert Richardson were at work, though in 1959 they were already abysmally behind even those times, as the young Anti-Uglies had rightly demonstrated.

Language, memory and construction

In these Hopkins buildings we find fact rather than the allusion of artifice, reality rather than premeditated dream, nearness rather than image. In a word, real imagination. We are relieved by a common sense and humanity all too lacking today when architecture is confused with fine art. Living architecture, like any useful art, does not mirror society but is a tool with which to shape it. But in the search for an appropriate architectural technology the idea of memory has to enter in. Again, referring to the Greek term *mnemotekne* (where *mneme* = memory) and their idea of 'systematic treatment', it becomes a matter of enlarging our present notion of science to embrace far more than matter. Nevertheless, the ordering device of any art form – painting, sculpture, literature, music – is always construction and that applies most of all to the mother art, which is about life. Amongst Auguste Perret's many dictums we find: 'Construction is the maternal language of architecture. An architect is a poet who thinks and talks in construction'. Mackintosh and Mendelsohn both subscribed to that belief and Hopkins, who has developed their traditions in terms of appropriate architectural technology, may also be considered the same type of poet: an architect of significant perception whose special and entirely professional contribution has been long awaited.

Auguste Perret:
Notre Dame du Raincy,
Paris, 1924.

Basildon Town Centre, 1981–

Basildon New Town in Essex was founded in 1949. By 1980 its population had reached 100,000. The shopping precinct in the centre of the town, built in the early 1960s, was no longer adequate and there were proposals for a large new covered shopping centre to be built in two phases towards the south-eastern perimeter of the town centre. The old precinct suffered from most of the environmental defects common to developments of its age and type. Its main open space, Town Square, was open, sparsely landscaped and inhospitable. The development corporation therefore commissioned Hopkins to prepare proposals for the improvement of the square, including roofing over the long rectangular space and providing a small number of new shops to finance the scheme.

Instead of a conventional steel and glass roof, Hopkins proposed a canopy of tensioned fabric. Permanent fabric structures were becoming common in the USA but were new to the UK. The practice was simultaneously developing the design of a fabric structure for the Schlumberger Cambridge Research Centre. In the case of Schlumberger, the fabric roof takes the form of three 'circus tents', with external steel frames lifting the fabric membrane high above the single-storey buildings on either side. In the Basildon scheme this arrangement is reversed. Rectangular, horizontal steel frames are suspended by tension rods, which form pairs of tubular-steel masts at regular centres along the square. A membrane of translucent Teflon-coated glass fibre is fitted to the edges of the frame and pulled downwards by tension rings around the masts to create a stable double-curved profile. The roof oversails the existing three and four-storey buildings on either side of the square, and the gap is closed by continuous horizontal vents. A glass wall at each end of the square completes the enclosure. Shops and small offices are located in simple two-storey buildings in the middle of the square, which is sheltered by the canopy.

The environment within the enclosure is controlled naturally. In summer the stack effect causes warm air to rise to the high-level louvres at the perimeter, pulling in fresh air from vents in the end walls. Solar heat gain is not critical since, unlike glass, the fabric permits long-wave radiation to escape to the atmosphere. In winter the enclosure gains heat from direct and diffuse short-wave solar radiation as well as benefiting from waste heat from the new and existing shops. The enclosure is big enough to be used as a reservoir of fresh air to ventilate the shops. Smoke ventilation in case of fire is also by non-mechanical means; the funnel-shaped roof directs smoke up to vents between the steel frames.

The scheme included proposals for large-scale landscaping, new graphics and signage and even, in one version, a cable-car ride suspended from the canopy structure.

174

Location plan

A lightweight fabric
membrane, divided into
15-metre bays, spans
the existing mall and is
tensioned beneath a
boom structure, the
double-curvature form
ensuring stiffness in
both directions.

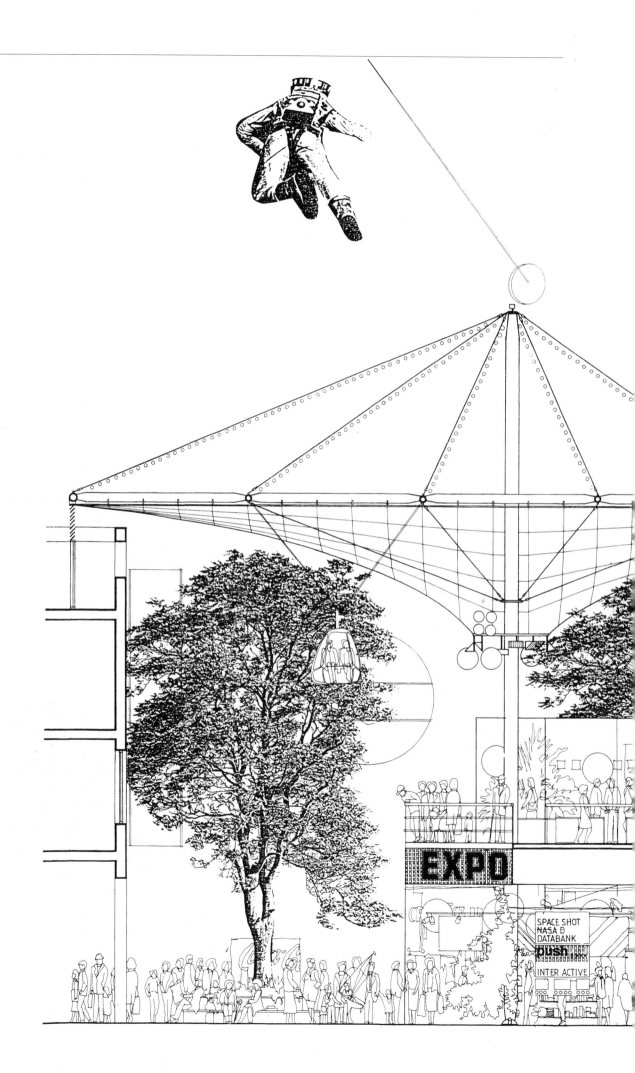

Section through Town Square

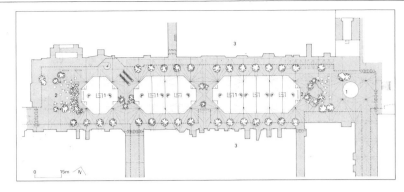

Plan
1 retail
2 cafe
3 existing retail

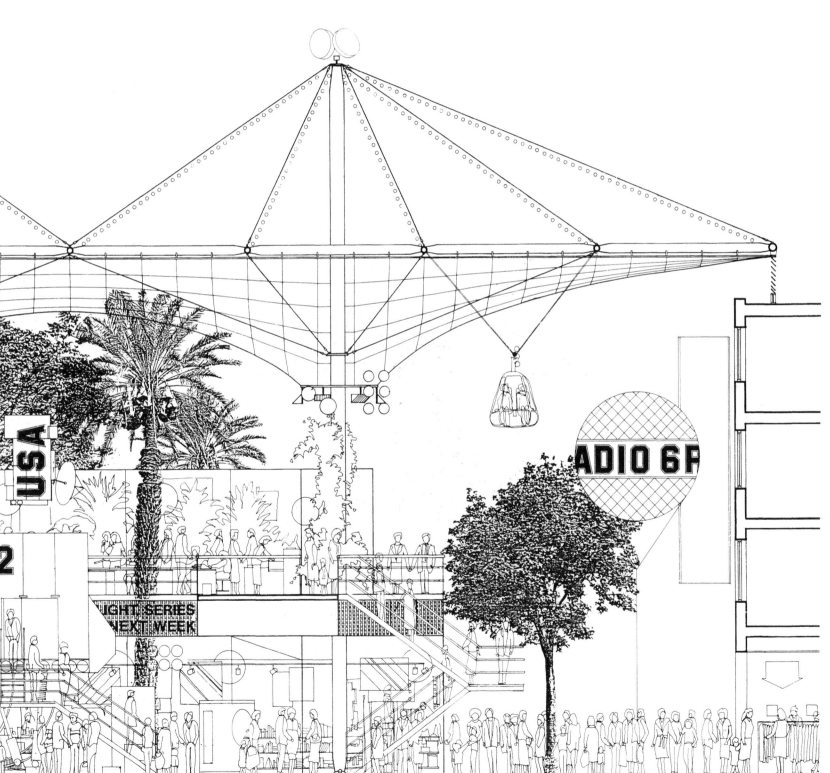

Hopkins designed a small
tented pavilion, which
was erected in Basildon
Town Square to show the
proposals.

Glyndebourne Opera House, 1989–1994

The Glyndebourne Opera House was founded in 1924 by John Christie. Built in the grounds of a country house, it has become a favourite summer attraction for opera lovers, who traditionally combine their visit with a lavish outdoor picnic in the long performance interval. Over the years the collection of buildings on the site has grown in an ad hoc fashion. In 1989 a report, entitled *Glyndebourne: Building an Independent Future,* recommended that a new, bigger theatre should be built in order to attract more revenue and safeguard the company's future.

Hopkins' design reorganises the accommodation on the site, reusing existing structures wherever possible. The main proposal, however, was for the demolition of the existing theatre and its replacement by a new building. A study of the existing site revealed an awkward, and inappropriate plan that tended to confuse front-of-house and backstage facilities. The solution was to turn the theatre round through 180 degrees.

This strategy had a number of advantages: the building could be dug into the natural slope of the site to reduce its impact on the landscape; the bulky fly tower could be set back so that it did not compete visually with the original country house; the new foyer could face the gardens used for picnics rather than the access road and the scenery dock could form part of a clearly defined 'industrial' zone away from the main public areas.

The proposed new building is a single volume, three storeys high and oval on plan with a shallow-pitched roof. Its traditional horseshoe auditorium is contained within a circular drum that projects above the main roof and is connected to the fly tower. A colonnade surrounds the front-of-house end of the building at ground level. This is extended radially on the axis to form a new glass-roofed foyer linking the new building to a restaurant in the refurbished shell of the old backstage block. The semicircular space behind the stage and fly tower provides a working and storage area, connected radially to the scenery get-in and to an acoustically isolated rehearsal block.

Offices for administrative and production staff are wrapped round the backstage part of the building so that their windows give a human scale to the otherwise large, blank volume. These rooms also serve as an acoustic buffer for the auditorium, and ensure that people who work all through the year at Glyndebourne have fresh air, daylight and views out. Dressing rooms, plant rooms, stores and workshops are in the basement.

The external walls are of brick, used not as cladding but as a true loadbearing material, with projecting piers and flat arched openings, exemplifying the way that the architectural character of a Hopkins building always arises naturally from the structural functions of its various elements.

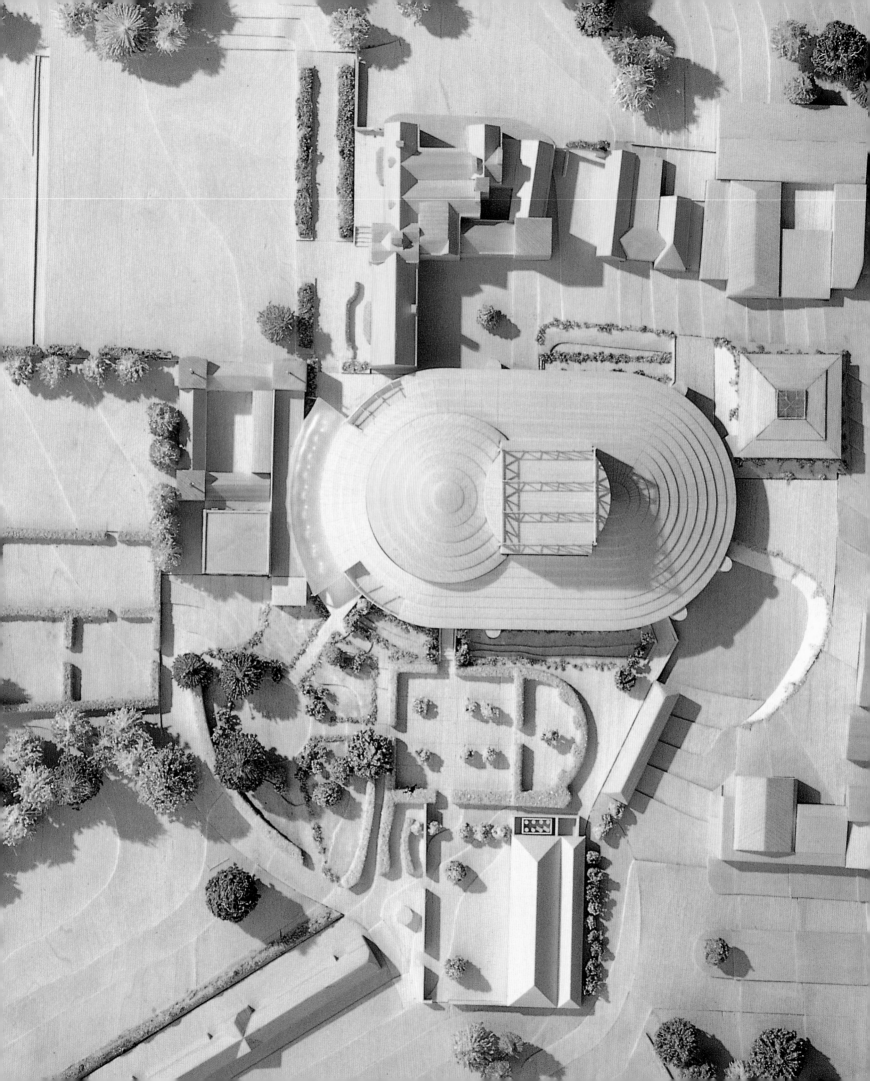

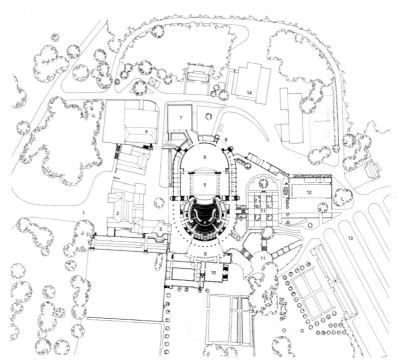

Site plan
1 entrance
2 house
3 organ room
4 Wallop's restaurant
5 stage
6 backstage
7 new rehearsal room
8 loading bay
9 foyer
10 old rehearsal stage
11 new gardens
12 new Mildmay Hall
13 car park
14 scenery store

Location plan

Hopkins' opera house
nestles among the
ensemble of existing
Glyndebourne buildings,
which help to mediate
between the new large
volumes and the
surrounding countryside.

Hopkins' new opera house is developed on the site of the old auditorium but its organisation is turned through 180 degrees. This allows the apparent bulk of the backstage areas to be reduced by digging into the natural slope of the site; and the height and volume of the fly tower is moved away from the main house. The new foyer is positioned on the garden front, naturally bringing the audience to the part of the site they have come to enjoy. The old dressing-room building remains will become part of a new restaurant next to the foyer.

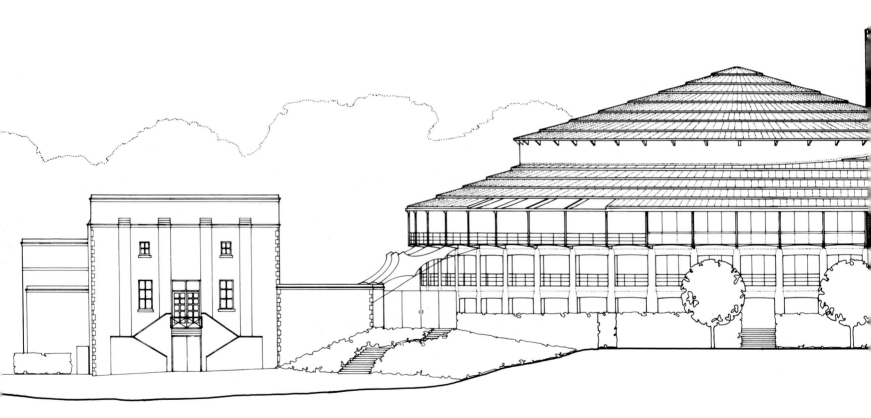

East elevation

New Parliamentary Building, 1989 –

This is the latest in a series of proposals to alleviate overcrowded conditions in the Palace of Westminster in London. The main purpose of the building is to provide offices for 208 MPs, but it will also accommodate the Committee Clerks' Department, a library, catering facilities and a suite of select committee rooms. The site, on the river frontage between the Palace of Westminster and a range of buildings by Norman Shaw, could hardly be more prominent or architecturally sensitive. It will form part of a 'parliamentary campus' with a secure perimeter stretching from Bridge Street to Richmond House and from Victoria Embankment to Parliament Street. Beneath the site lies Westminster underground station, which will be redesigned for London Transport with a new ticket hall below ground.

The basic form of the proposed building is very simple – a six-storey rectangular block with a central courtyard. An arcade extends at ground-floor level along the two street frontages, sheltering the station entrance flanked by a pair of shops on the Bridge Street side, and the main public entrance to the building on the Victoria Embankment side. The entrance hall gives direct access, via a grand staircase, to the committee rooms on the first floor. For MPs, however, the main entrance is via an existing pedestrian subway that crosses Bridge Street from New Palace Yard and rises via escalators in the central courtyard. The courtyard is surrounded at ground level and first-floor levels by cloister-like corridors. At second-floor level the courtyard is covered with a spectacular arched glass roof so that it becomes a landscaped conservatory with a bar, a cafeteria and a library reading area.

Above the level of the courtyard roof, the cloister arrangement gives way to a conventional plan with a central corridor serving cellular offices. This means that the building can be mainly naturally lit, with a consequent saving in energy costs. Ventilation is provided by air shafts on the facade, connecting the individual rooms to tall chimneys on the roof. Fans housed in the roof space exhaust stale air through the chimneys and draw in fresh air at the bases of the shafts through heat-recovery units.

The chimneys are functional elements, not mere decoration, but the picturesque roofline they create is one of a number of features that help to reconcile the new building with its sensitive context. The texture of the stone and bronze facades echoes the Perpendicular Gothic decoration of the Palace of Westminster, the curved corners recall the turrets of the Norman Shaw Buildings, and the black-patinated bronze roof panels have been selected to match the roofs of both neighbours. Hopkins' aim has been to create a work of architecture that will sit comfortably in its historic setting, but at the same time provide all the facilities and energy efficiency expected of a late 20th century building.

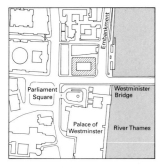

Location plan

Hopkins' New Parliamentary Building adopts a courtyard form, providing maximum exterior frontage lined with committee rooms and individual offices for Members and their staff on the upper floors. The central courtyard will be enclosed with a glazed roof to shelter restaurant and reading room facilities on the ground floor.

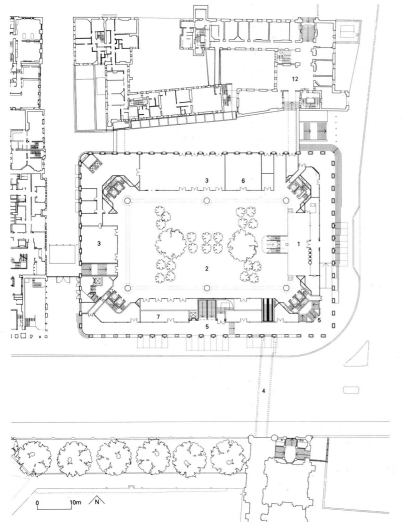

Ground floor plan

First floor plan

Floor plans

1 main entrance
2 covered courtyard
3 restaurant
4 subway to Palace of Westminster
5 Westminster underground

station entrance
6 library
7 retail
8 clerks' department
9 select committee
10 meeting
11 members and staff

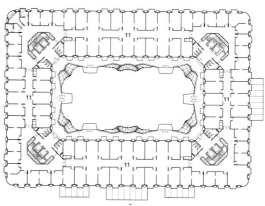

Upper floor plan

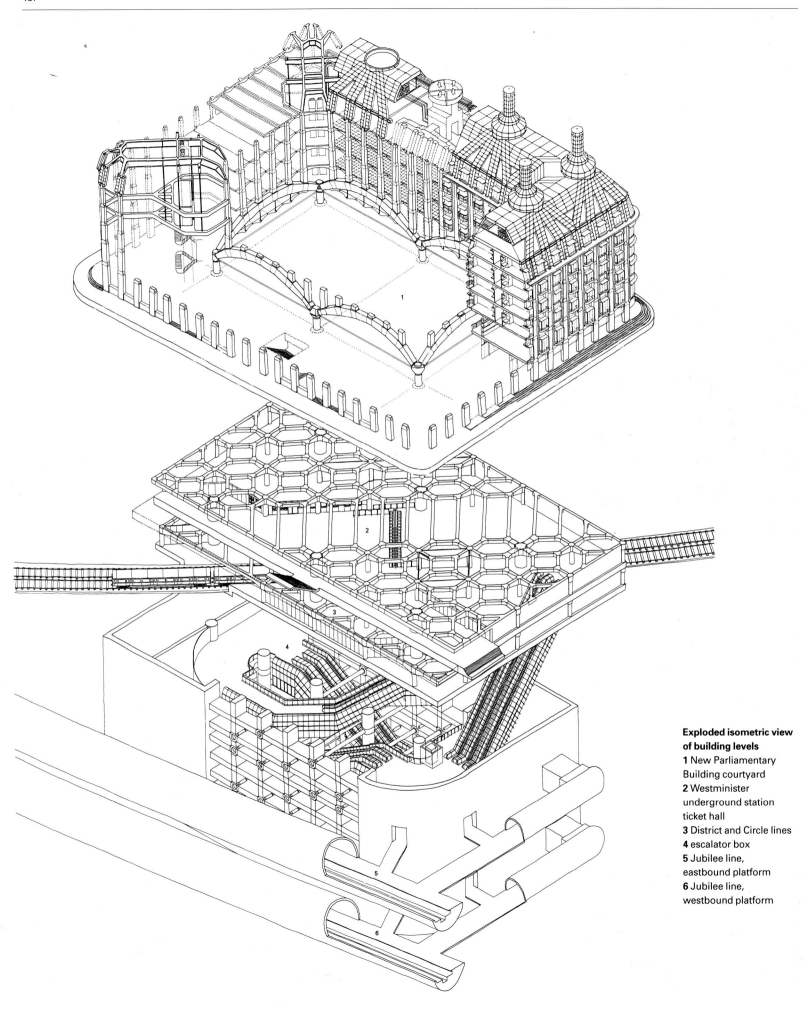

Exploded isometric view of building levels
1 New Parliamentary Building courtyard
2 Westminister underground station ticket hall
3 District and Circle lines
4 escalator box
5 Jubilee line, eastbound platform
6 Jubilee line, westbound platform

Hopkins' building is
characterised by clarity
in the use of materials:
the stone piers are
loadbearing, bronze air
shafts connect individual
rooms to the chimneys on
the roof, and light shelves
are used to direct daylight
as far into the occupied
space as possible.

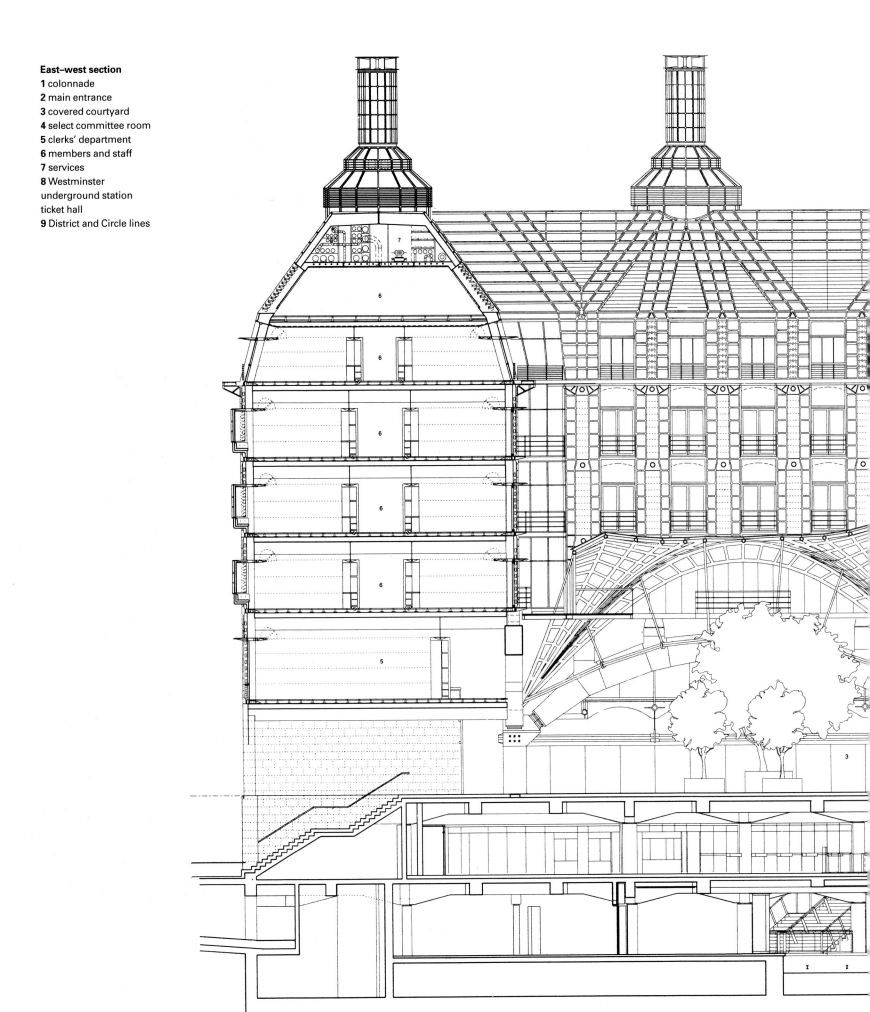

East–west section
1 colonnade
2 main entrance
3 covered courtyard
4 select committee room
5 clerks' department
6 members and staff
7 services
8 Westminster
underground station
ticket hall
9 District and Circle lines

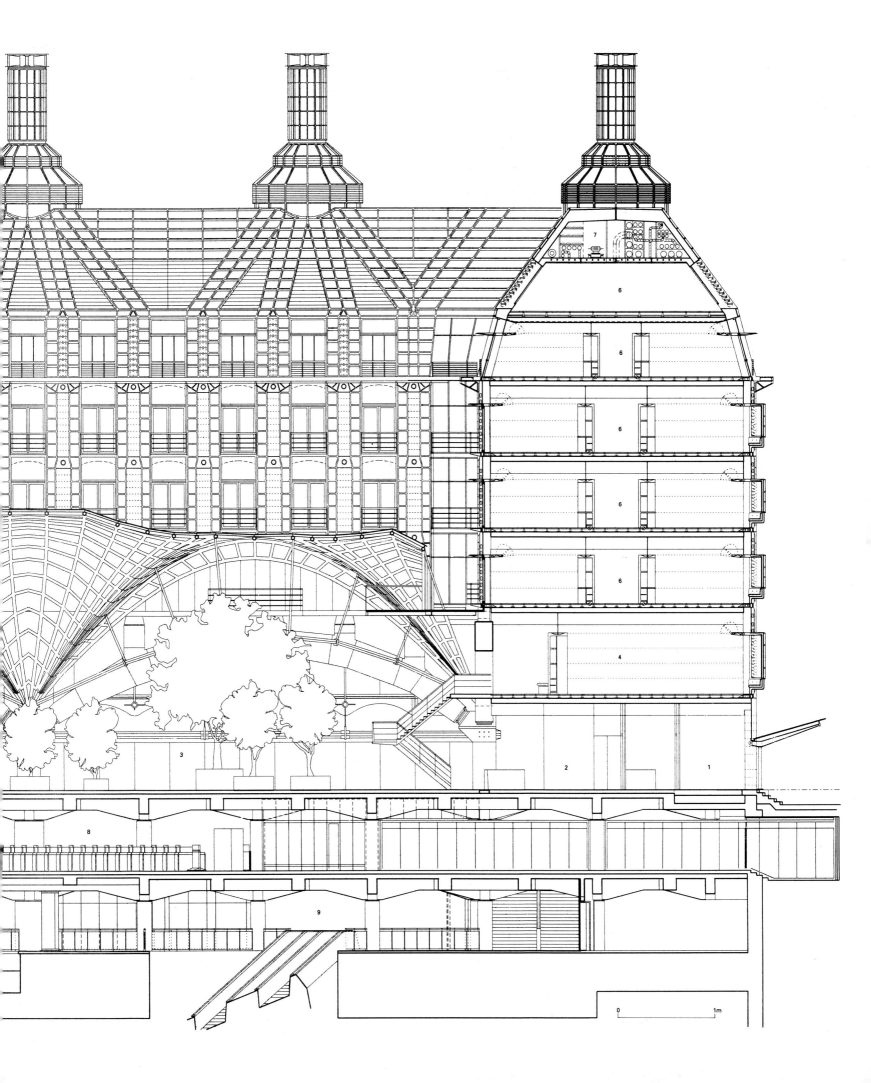

0   1m

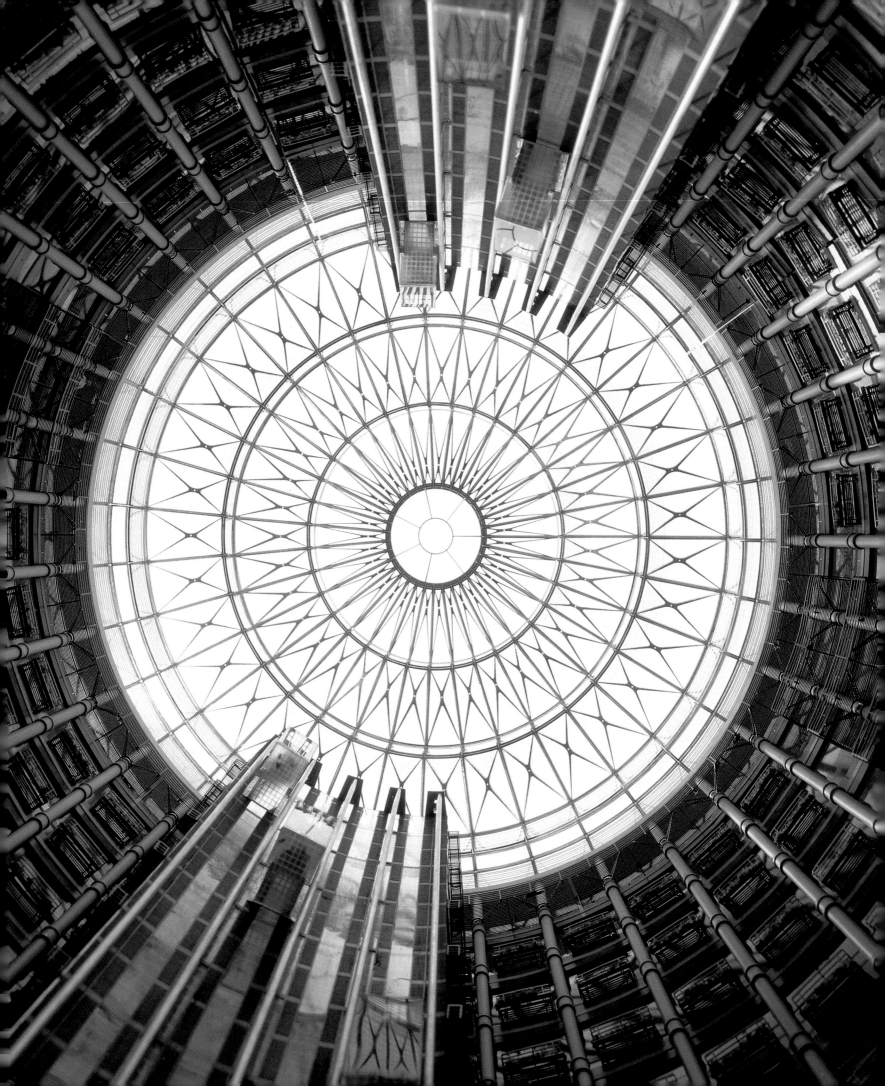

Marylebone Gate Office Development, 1989 –

This project arose from the coincidence of British Rail's decision to restructure the railway lines at London's Marylebone Station and the purchase by a property company of the leasehold of Melbury House, a 12-storey 1960s' office block on an adjacent site to the north. This presented the opportunity for a joint redevelopment of the site, which would provide new offices and rejuvenate the existing station buildings. The brief that resulted from this collaboration called for a seven-storey office building to replace Melbury House, a block of flats to the north on the site of a smaller existing office building and the refurbishment of the station forecourt.

The proposed office building is of a size and scale to match the dominant building in the area, the Windsor Hotel, which occupies a complete city block between Marylebone Road and the station forecourt. Like the hotel, the office block is almost square on plan, with the west side slightly angled to align with Harewood Avenue. Although each of the four aspects of the building is different, with the station concourse to the south, the railway lines to the east, the residential area to the north and Harewood Avenue to the west, the facades are almost identical and the plan has a diagrammatic simplicity: a circle within a square, with a superimposed diagonal cross to define the secondary circulation routes. The circle is a top-lit atrium, overlooked by a ring of cellular offices surrounded by the main circulation route. The majority of the lettable office space forms a continuous band around this zone. Service cores, containing escape stairs, goods lifts, wcs and stores, are placed internally in the four corners where the plan is deepest. Secondary, radial, circulation routes bisect the cores and link the quadrant-shaped corners of the building with four lift towers, which project into the atrium.

The main entrance, with a glazed canopy, is in the middle of the Harewood Avenue facade but there is a second entrance from the station concourse. This sets up a symbiotic relationship between the office building and the station. It is envisaged that most of the users of the office building will arrive by train, reducing the need for car parking. There is, however, a basement car park. Most of the mechanical plant is also housed in the basement in order to reduce the height of the building. The external walls take the form of loadbearing frames, with hollow columns at close centres clearly expressed. These convey fresh air to the basement plant. Steel and ceramic tiles are the main materials, reflecting the cast iron and faience of the station and hotel.

The access road also serves the basement car park of the proposed six-storey residential block. This forms a transition in scale between the large, commercial and public buildings to the south of the site, and the housing estate of mainly three- and four-storey buildings to the north.

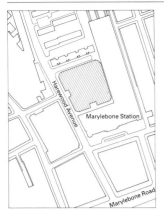

Location plan

Floor plans
1 Marylebone Station
2 station forecourt
3 entrance to underground station
4 offices
5 entrance to office building
6 atrium
7 lifts
8 office cores
9 ramp to underground car park
10 new residential units

Upper floor plan

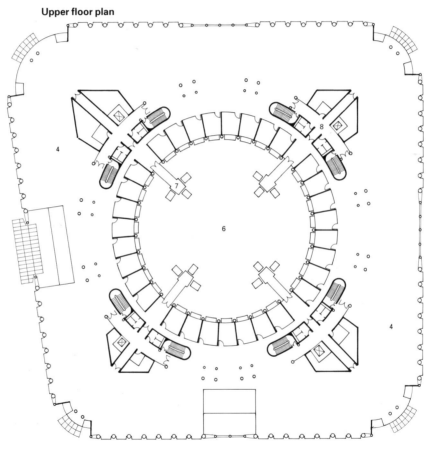

The building relates closely to the existing station, occupying a site formerly taken up by railway tracks and an outdated office building; it will be possible for office workers travelling by train to enter the building directly from the station concourse.

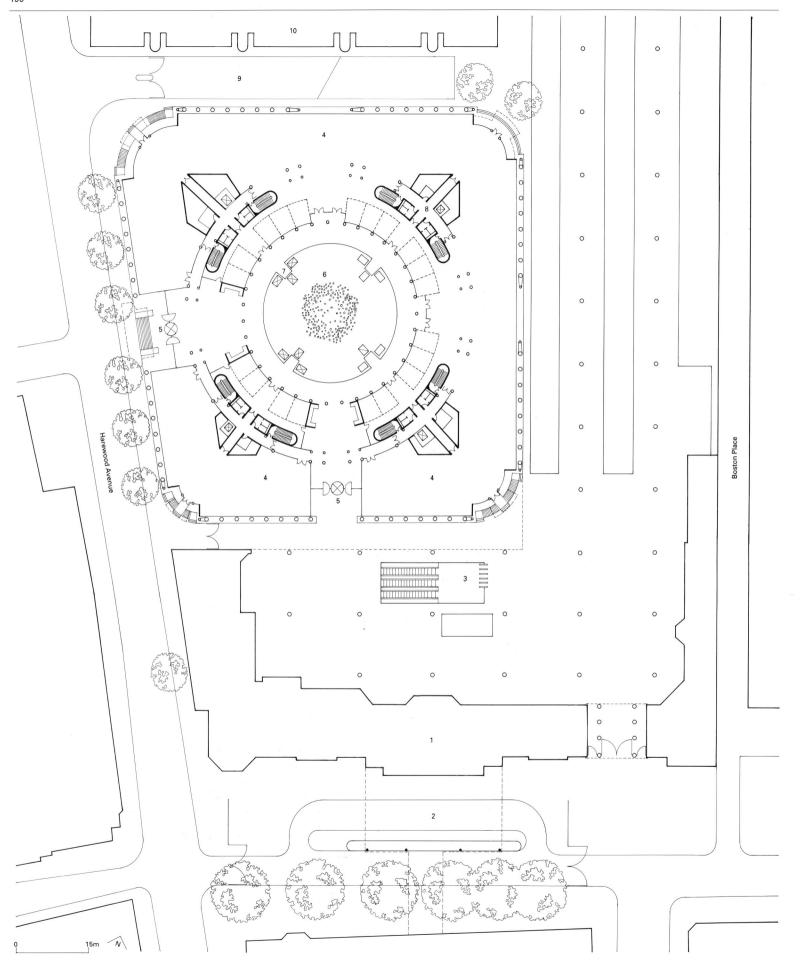

Ground floor plan

A circular, top-lit atrium forms the dominant organisational and spatial element in the plan. Rising through nine levels it is overlooked by a ring of cellular offices on each floor.

Tottenham Court Road Station, 1990 –

St Giles Circus is one of the most congested places in central London, especially for pedestrians. Tottenham Court Road underground station, which serves both the Central and Northern lines, lies beneath the road junction, and has cramped entrances from the pavements on all four street corners. London Regional Transport's main aim in asking Hopkins to prepare proposals for the development of the site on the south-western corner was to relieve the congestion in the station and upgrade it to serve two new routes: Crossrail and the Chelsea to Hackney line. The new building will also provide shops, offices and leisure facilities.

As well as improving the environment for pedestrians and rail travellers, the building has another important public function: to re-establish the civic dignity of what is in effect the eastern gateway of London's main shopping district.

Hopkins' proposal involves the complete demolition of the existing buildings which, though within a conservation area, are of no particular architectural merit. The key to the planning strategy is a diagonal pedestrian short-cut through the middle of the site in the form of an arcade inspired by Sicilian Avenue, which is a local landmark. Like the avenue, the proposed arcade is traffic-free and lined with shops and restaurants. Unlike Sicilian Avenue, however, it is covered and opens out in the middle from a top-lit atrium overlooked by the five office floors above. The main station ticket hall occupies a large oval space beneath the floor of the atrium, and is entered via escalators from the Oxford Street and Charing Cross Road corner, where there is also a third ground-level entrance to the arcade. There are other station entrances via staircases at each end of the arcade. A jazz club at sub-basement level beneath the ticket hall replaces the existing amenity of the Astoria theatre.

The plan is clearly legible; it is basically symmetrical about a diagonal north-east to south-west axis. This legibility is reinforced by the unified, castle-like external form with four cylindrical corner towers. The biggest of these towers, on the Oxford Street and Charing Cross Road corner, marks the main entrance to the station and contains a continuous spiral ramp that will be used as a public art gallery. Two smaller towers contain mechanical plant and hover over the entrances to the arcade. The fourth tower, on the south-west corner, marks the entrance to the offices and contains circular conference rooms.

Shopfronts at ground level around the perimeter of the building are sheltered by a continuous glass awning, linking the three public entrances. Most of the vertical structure is concentrated at the perimeter of the building to keep foundations clear of the many underground structures. External walls are mostly glass, with exposed metal columns at close centres corresponding to the width of the cellular offices.

Floor plans
1 entrance to
underground station
2 new arcade
3 retail
4 office entrance
5 jazz club entrance
6 gallery entrance
7 service area
8 Centre Point
9 new ticket hall
10 link to existing
ticket hall
11 Crossrail escape stairs
12 escalators to Crossrail
and Northern line
13 escalators to Central
line and Chelsea–
Hackney line
14 ancillary
accommodation
15 office
16 atrium
17 conference tower
18 plant tower
19 gallery tower

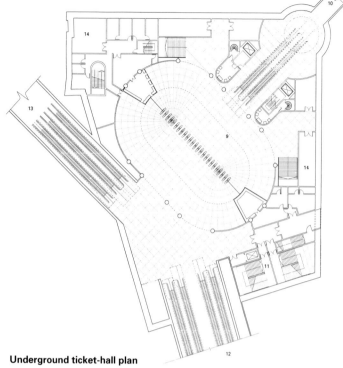

Underground ticket-hall plan

Location plan

The plan is organised
symmetrically about
a diagonal axis
and interweaves a
network of pedestrian
routes and public spaces
at a variety of levels.

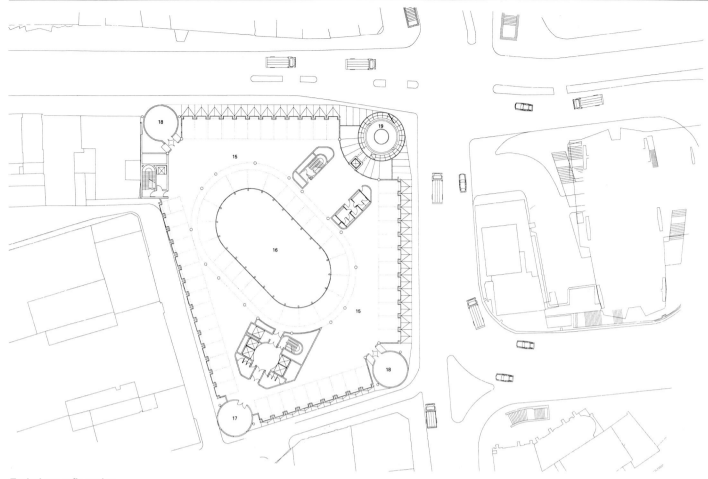

Typical upper floor plan

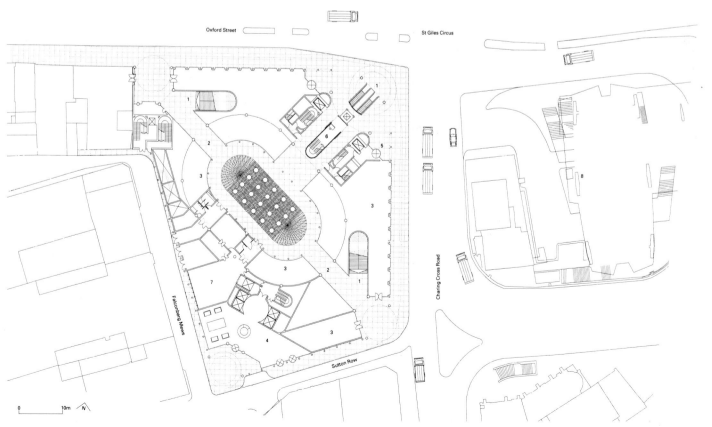

Oxford Street

St Giles Circus

Falconberg Mews

Charing Cross Road

Sutton Row

0   10m

Ground floor plan

The largest of the
building's three towers,
on the corner of Oxford
Street and Charing Cross
Road, signals the main
entrance to the
underground station
and features in its
upper floors a spiral
ramp, which will form
a public art gallery.

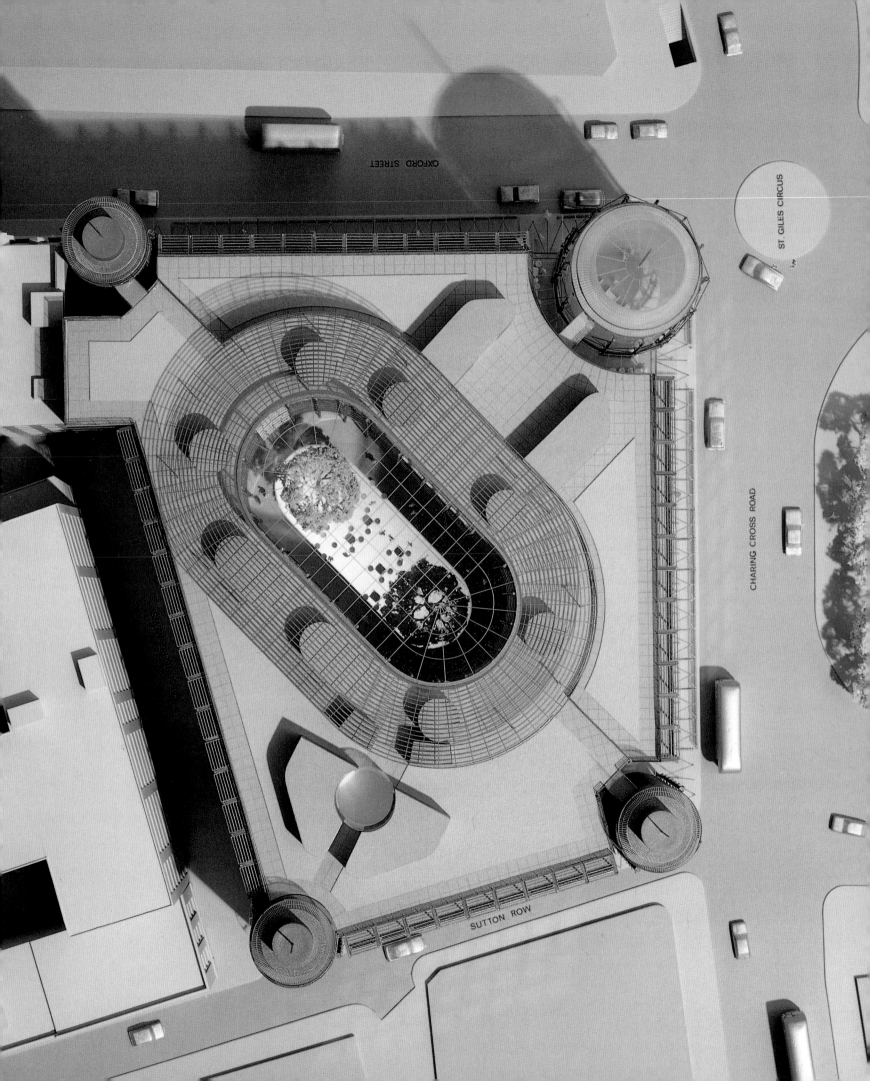

OXFORD STREET

ST. GILES CIRCUS

CHARING CROSS ROAD

SUTTON ROW

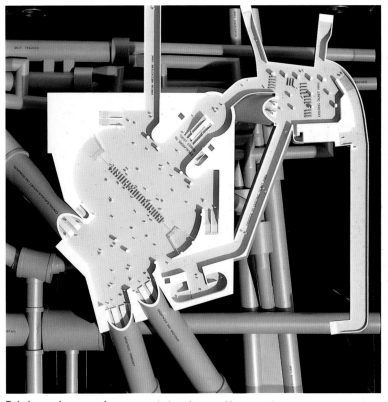

Existing and proposed underground structures, such as ticket halls, escalator and train tunnels, ventilation shafts and sewers, imposed severe constraints in development on the site; they precluded the use of deep-piled foundations and limited the loads that the substructure could bear. These constraints, coupled with the organisational and safety restrictions imposed by the new station layout, meant that the number of internal columns within the new ticket hall had to be minimised. As a result, the perimeter walls of the ticket hall and the building above align vertically and therefore carry a substantial proportion of the structural loads, which are transferred to the ground via the station floor raft.

Younger Universe, 1990–

The Younger Universe site was given to the City of Edinburgh by the Scottish and Newcastle Brewery on condition that it be developed for public use and bear the company name 'Younger'. It is one of three adjacent sites in the Old Town, close to the Royal Mile, which were vacated by the brewery when it moved out of town. The remaining two sites will be developed for a mixture of commercial and residential uses.

The Royal Mile, which connects the castle with the Palace of Holyroodhouse, is the main tourist axis of the city. Hopkins' brief was to design a new attraction in the form of a 'black box' to house a permanent exhibition telling the story of the creation and evolution of the planet Earth. There are three main elements in the design: a circular forecourt and dropping-off point for coaches; a two-storey building containing the exhibition itself, with administrative offices, stores and workshops, and a rooftop pavilion enclosed by a glass wall and fabric canopy. In addition, a basement car park extends across the whole site, entered via a new road on the west side. The main entrance to the exhibition is through the rooftop pavilion, which is reached from the forecourt via a stepped amphitheatre.

Like the Mound Stand at Lord's and the David Mellor Factory at Hathersage, the starting point for the design was an existing structure, in this case the remains of the stone wall that was once part of the original brewery, including a castle-like tower on the south-eastern corner. This wall, restored and extended, forms the external wall of the black box.

Offices and workshops are ranged on either side of the exhibition space, which erupts through the roof, under the fabric canopy, in the form of a hemispherical dome over a multi-media theatre. Although the space under the canopy is completely enclosed, it has a quasi-external character and is unheated. Two more structures emerge from the building below, each containing a small catering facility as well as a lift and a pair of spiral staircases leading down to the exhibition. The rooftop pavilion therefore combines the functions of entrance hall, cafe and observation platform, with spectacular views over Holyrood Park. When viewed from the road on the northern side, the flamboyant canopy, suspended by cables from steel masts is silhouetted against the backdrop of Arthur's Seat and Salisbury Crags.

The forecourt is a truly monumental urban space, despite its mundane function as a short-stay coach park. A long, curving ramp on one side provides access for disabled people. Trees planted in a regular, radial pattern enhance the feeling of enclosure, and a new pedestrian avenue connects the space to the Palace of Holyroodhouse. The centre of the forecourt will be equipped with a fountain, but it might occasionally become a stage for open-air theatrical performances, especially during the Edinburgh Festival.

Location plan

Above a basement car park, which covers the site, the scheme comprises three principal elements: a grand circular forecourt, a two-storey block containing the exhibition and associated facilities, and a rooftop pavilion sheltered beneath a familiar fabric canopy. Hopkins' building occupies a key position on the Royal Mile close to Holyroodhouse in Edinburgh's main tourist centre, and houses a new exhibition relating the story of the earth's creation.

Long section

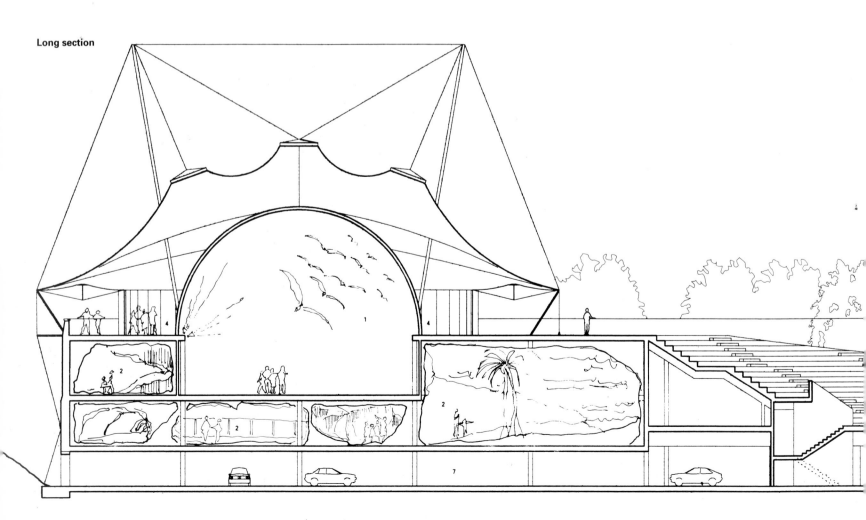

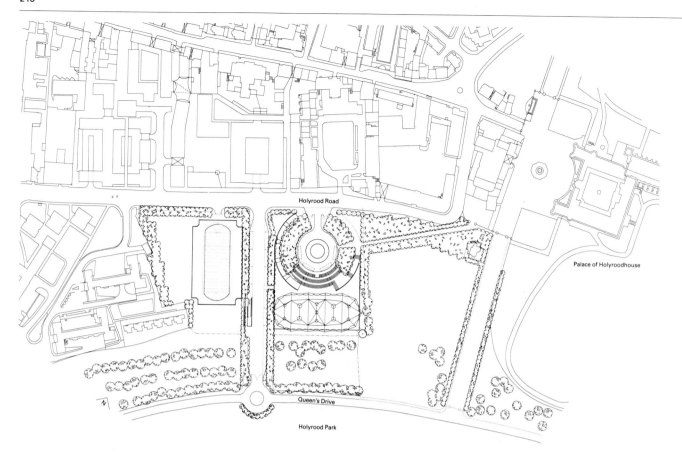

Holyrood Road

Palace of Holyroodhouse

Queen's Drive

Holyrood Park

Sections
1 auditorium
2 exhibition
3 administration/
kitchen/wcs
4 visitor concourse
5 shop
6 cafeteria
7 car park

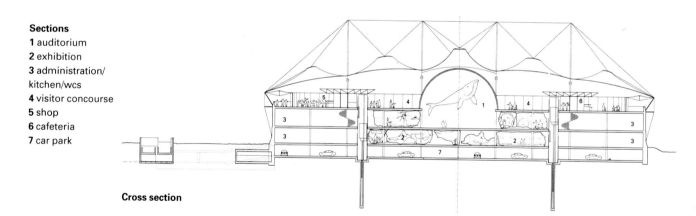

Cross section

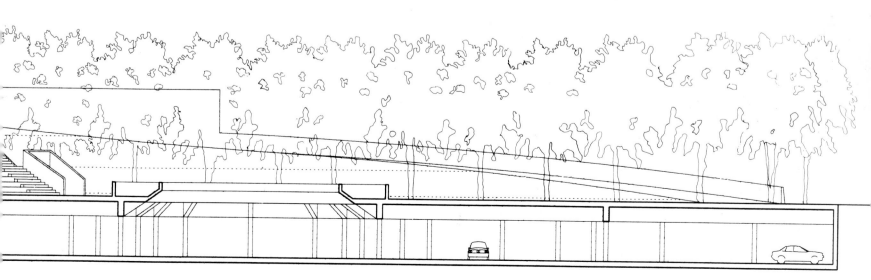

Ostensibly a short-stay coach park, the Younger Universe forecourt is a monumentally scaled civic gesture, creating a new urban space on the Royal Mile. Entry to the exhibition is via the rooftop pavilion, which is reached by a ramp or the amphitheatre steps in the forecourt.

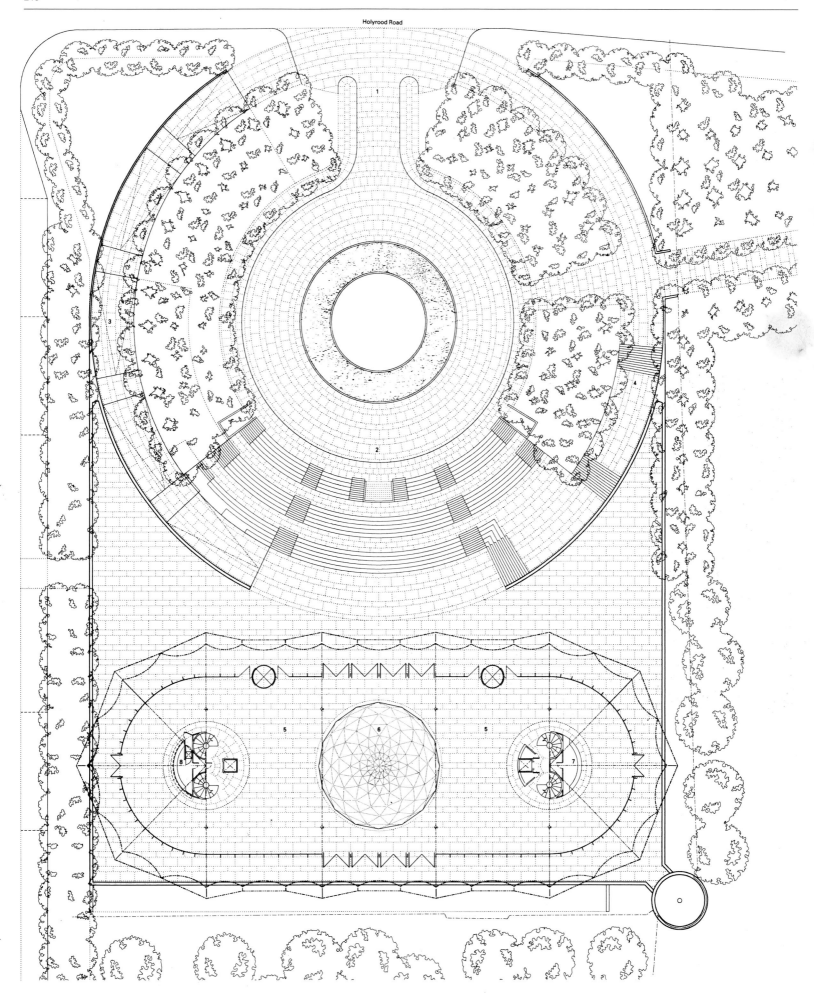

Holyrood Road

Victoria Transport Interchange, 1991–

Victoria Station was built 20 years before the invention of the motor car. In the years since then, the station surroundings have been adapted in an ad hoc fashion to the requirements of buses, taxis, service vehicles and private cars. In the process, the pedestrian has been forgotten.

The main aim of this project is to improve the environment for pedestrians and public transport users. In order to pay for these improvements the scheme includes two large new office buildings. All existing buildings between the station front and Victoria Street are to be demolished to allow a complete reorganisation of the forecourt and the underground station below. Central to the plan is a new bus station, which has a curving, steel and glass canopy, linking the station access road to Victoria Street.

The human scale of this relatively low structure softens the impact of the office buildings on either side. One of these, between the bus station and Buckingham Palace Road, is an eight-storey building with shops, a service bay and an underground station entrance on the ground floor. Its footprint is determined by the site boundary, and its height by the adjacent hotel and other buildings. The main entrance, on the north-eastern corner, opens into a full-height, top-lit atrium. Cylindrical towers at the remaining three corners contain additional services and plant. The other office building is a 22-storey tower with a teardrop-shaped plan and a stepped profile. Its form and siting are dramatic,

but derived mainly from functional considerations. Most pedestrians leaving the station walk towards Victoria Street. In order to ease the rush-hour congestion, the office building has been placed some distance from the front of the station, creating a wide piazza and opening up views of the station facades. This brings it into line with Victoria Street, which is kinked northwards at this point. It is therefore able to perform an important townscape function, closing the vista along one of Westminster's main thoroughfares and signalling the presence of the transport interchange. The plan is symmetrical, with the main entrance placed on axis, facing up Victoria Street. Its streamlined shape and the windguards around the facade are designed to reduce the risk of creating a windy microclimate on the piazza.

The building's cutaway profile also has a programmatic justification. The placing of piles is restricted by the undergound tunnels beneath the site and the resulting foundation plan dictates that loads should be concentrated at the western or 'stern' end of the building. The 'prow' is therefore lightened by two five-storey atriums and the progressive set back of the upper floors. A continuous, 8 metre-high 'pile cap' projects 4 metres above the ground to form the external wall at piazza level. Above this, the external walls are akin to those of the other office building, with metal columns at 3 metre centres on storey-height, splayed metal castings.

Location plan

Floor plans
1 Victoria Station
2 Grosvenor Hotel
3 new bus station
4 piazza
5 building reception
6 service yard
7 retail units
8 restaurant
9 bus station roof
10 office
11 void

At the centre of the
Hopkins plan, between
the new buildings, is
a bus station whose
curving steel and glass
canopy links the
station access road
to Victoria Street.

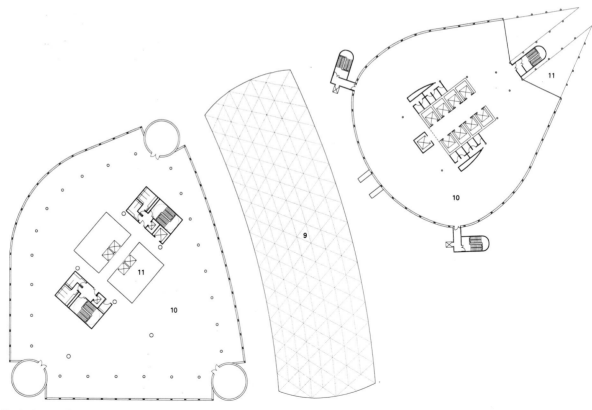

Typical upper floor plan

Ground floor plan

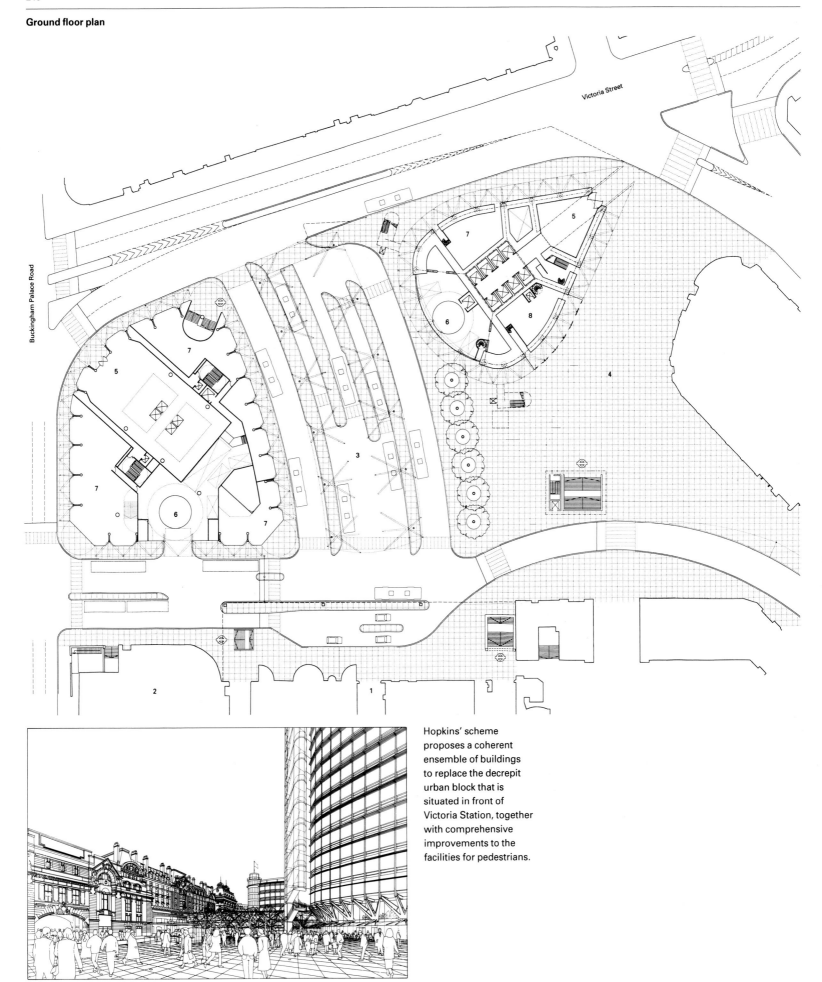

Victoria Street

Buckingham Palace Road

Hopkins' scheme proposes a coherent ensemble of buildings to replace the decrepit urban block that is situated in front of Victoria Station, together with comprehensive improvements to the facilities for pedestrians.

The office tower provides
an urban focus for the
scheme; its distinctive
tear-drop profile closes
the long vista from
Victoria Street and signals
the station's presence.

New Inland Revenue Centre, 1992–1994

The Inland Revenue's original intention to build a new centre in Nottingham on a 'design and build' basis met with an outcry from the architectural profession and the disapproval of local planners. This led to a change of policy and an architectural competition was launched, which attracted 130 entries. Hopkins was the eventual winner.

The derelict, hinterland site, close to the city centre, is bounded by a canal to the north and a railway line to the south. The scheme aims to extend the urban grain of the city southwards. A gently curving east–west boulevard is intersected by radiating streets. The three and four-storey office buildings form traditional city blocks enclosing gardens. Cars are parked in the tree-lined streets. The site plan is basically symmetrical, with common facilities, including a sports hall and a restaurant, at the centre of the development within a fabric-roofed structure.

The office buildings are designed with two main aims in mind: to control the internal environment by passive means, using the minimum of mechanical plant, and to use local, traditional materials, engineered in a modern way. Natural lighting and ventilation preclude the use of deep plans. Office wings are only 13.6 metres deep, with an offset central circulation route to allow cellular and open-plan accommodation. Vertical circulation is by helical staircases in glazed, cylindrical towers at the corners of the blocks. These form an important part of the natural ventilation system. Warm air is drawn from the office areas into the towers through full-height doors and travels up the open stairwell to vents in the roof. This flow is assisted in summer by the natural stack effect caused by solar heat gain, and in winter by wind acting on the adjustable vents. Fresh air is introduced through ordinary opening windows and vents into the raised floors. There is no air conditioning and heating is by low-pressure, hot-water radiators. Maximum use is made of daylight, via 'light shelves' over the windows. These shade the windows from intrusive sunshine and reflect the light upwards onto the curved, concrete soffit.

In order to achieve the high thermal mass required by the passive environmental design, construction is mainly of heavy materials. Precast concrete floor units act as a folded plate and span the full width of the blocks; they sit on loadbearing piers of Nottingham semi-engineering bricks. The form of these piers responds to structural demands, the section footprint reducing as the loads diminish on the upper levels. The top floor jetties out 1.2 metres. Steel trusses support a roof covering of lead-clad, plywood panels.

This project has an importance beyond the immediate requirements of the client and the City of Nottingham as it represents a new alternative to the deep-plan, air-conditioned, high-energy consumption office buildings designed in the 1980s.

Location plan

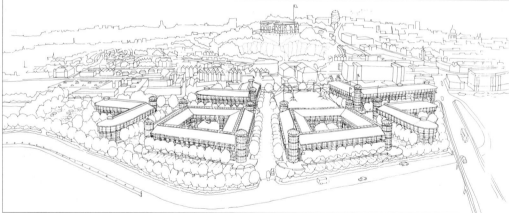

The Inland Revenue's new buildings occupy a formerly derelict industrial site in Nottingham, bounded on one side by a canal and on the other by a railway line. From this unpromising context, Hopkins' scheme sets out to recreate the urban grain of the city centre, notionally moving the boundary of the central area southwards. Within the site, a new boulevard curves from east to west, forming new city blocks as it intersects with a series of streets laid out in a radial pattern whose focus is the castle.

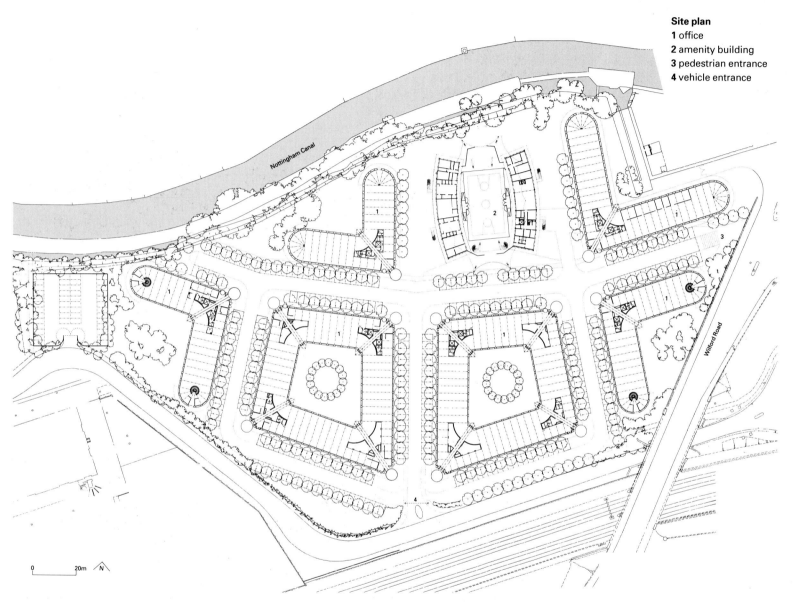

Site plan
1 office
2 amenity building
3 pedestrian entrance
4 vehicle entrance

Nottingham Canal

Wilford Road

0   20m   N

Cylindrical stair towers at the corners of the office blocks also form a strategic part of the building's natural ventilation system: exhaust air is drawn into the towers from the office floors and is taken up the stairwell to vents in the roof.

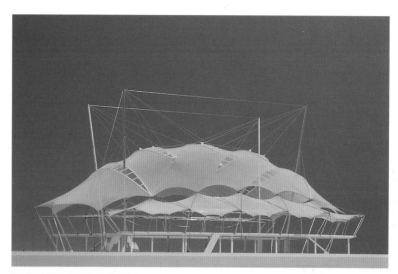

A fabric-roofed amenity
building is located at the
heart of the site. It takes
the form of a curvilinear
two-storey building
with accommodation
arranged around a central
covered space and
contains a sports hall,
multi-gym, restaurant
and nursery.

Towards a New Tectonic

Kenneth Frampton

Hopkins House,
Hampstead,
London, 1976.

Michael and Patty Hopkins' independent career began with the design and realisation of their own lightweight modular house, built in Hampstead, London, in 1976. From the point of view of its constructive rationale, this all-metal, two-storey dwelling represents an advance over Charles Eames' pioneering modular house of 1949. Comparable in profile with Craig Ellwood's Case Study House in Beverly Hills of 1958, this house is inflected by an asymmetrical approach bridge from the street that serves to articulate its minimalist High-Tech, and takes the form of a 12 metre by 10 metre envelope subdivided into six 2 metre modules in width and five in depth. As Patty Hopkins explains: 'There was no question but that it would be built with metal and glass because this was seen as an opportunity to refine and reduce in scale techniques developed for larger commercial buildings. Structural members and junctions were to be small and repetitive. Floors and walls were to be thin membranes and expressed as such in their end conditions ... A small grid of 4 metres by 2 metres was chosen, which kept the structural sections small and enabled secondary structures to be eliminated. Perimeter columns are ... used directly as cladding and glazing supports. Internally there are eight columns which modulate space, provide the opportunity for subdivision and yet are small enough not to interrupt the space when subdivision is not required.'[1]

Despite its want of thermal mass, the simplicity of this house, plus the evident logic of its assembly led to a series of interesting commissions. Among them were two significant works both built in Bury St Edmunds: an almost identical metal house and a racking plant for the brewers Greene King, completed in 1980. Like the Hopkins House, Greene King is a well-serviced, ribbed metal shed lightly poised on the ground and raised on short concrete piles about 90cm above the surrounding flood plain; an obligatory elevation that simultaneously provided for the convenient loading of flat-bed trucks at either end of the shed. As with their own house, a lattice truss serves, through its inter-columnar supports, to subdivide the available floor space into zones for loading, washing, filling, storage and so on. The full width of the shed comprises three 24 metre bays and two 2 metre gangways running down the shed on either side, affording permanent access between the ends. In the longitudinal direction there are six 16 metre bays and two 8 metre overhangs at either end to provide shelter for loading. What gives this building its elegance is the simplicity of the fundamental components from which it is made, the continuous concrete floor slab elevated on piles, the lightweight truss designed by the engineer Anthony Hunt and the horizontal, profiled metal cladding that encloses the structure together with the standard up-and-over glazed, garage doors on the ends. All these elements, plus stanchions at 8 metre intervals to secure the cladding, make this well-serviced shed seem like a silver pagoda, which unexpectedly emerges from the East Anglian countryside.

Any assessment of the work of Michael Hopkins and Partners cannot be isolated from those formative years between 1969 and 1975, which Hopkins spent as a partner of Norman Foster, taking the design lead on such works as the IBM headquarters at Cosham, realised by Foster Associates in 1971. It is evident that Hopkins went in a certain direction because of this experience not only from his own Greene King plant but also from the next major commission to come into the office, the 1981 proposal to throw a lightweight tent over the main square

Greene King Draught
Beer Cellars, Bury St
Edmunds, Suffolk, 1980.

in Basildon New Town. The Basildon proposal clearly owed much to the pioneering work of Frei Otto and to SOM's Haj Terminal at Jeddah in Saudi Arabia of 1978, not to mention Foster's own proposal for an air-supported structure over a perimeter office complex at Hammersmith Broadway, designed for London Transport in 1978. Hopkins' 45 metre by 15 metre, mast-supported tent modules projected for Basildon were destined to become the trial run for the Schlumberger Cambridge Research Centre of 1982 and for the Mound Stand at Lord's, constructed in London five years later.

Between Basildon and Schlumberger came the important Patera lightweight factory system developed as a universal, modular building kit for the young entrepreneur Nigel Dale. Inspired by a prefabricated building tradition that goes back to the Crystal Palace, the now-abandoned Patera system continues to be of interest for two main reasons: firstly, for its strategic distinction between the 'soft/wet' site works and the 'hard/dry' mechanical character of the system itself, and, secondly, for the brilliant contribution of the project team, led by John Pringle with engineer Mark Whitby, which resulted in the ingenious hinged, hybrid frame, designed as a welded tubular, exoskeletal truss with a compression-free upper chord. Under dead loading, this acts as a three-hinged portal frame, with its central tie in the upper truss remaining slack. With snow pressure this tie loosens, enabling the lower chord of the truss to go into compression. With wind uplift, the tie again goes into tension while the coupled knee joint comes into play to carry the corresponding compression around the bend. Under these conditions the portal then acts as a two-hinged frame. The truss is made of machine-tooled, lightweight, welded components that can be readily transhipped and assembled. Since the structure is on the exterior there is no need to protect it from fire. Patera was also exceptional for the integration of services into its membrane, for its ingenious waterproofing and for its pressed sheet steel, insulated cladding.

The spirit of Patera carried over into the next major commission, the Schlumberger Cambridge Research Laboratories, commissioned at the end of 1982 and built

Top left, SOM: Haj Terminal, Jeddah, Saudi Arabia, 1980.
Top right, Frei Otto and Günter Behnisch: Olympic stadium, Munich, Germany, 1972.
Bottom, Basildon Town Centre, Essex, 1981.

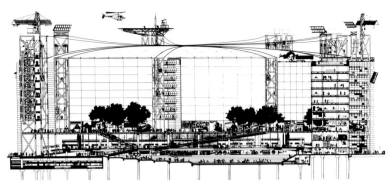

outside Cambridge in 1985. Like the Mound Stand that followed, this was an exercise in mixed-media construction. However, where the Mound Stand combined tented construction with traditional masonry, Schlumberger interfaced its three-bay tent, hung from an exoskeletal frame with a modular office system based on Patera. Schlumberger belongs to a whole generation of High-Tech, long-span sheds with cable-stayed lightweight roofs supported by exoskeletal frames; for example, Foster's Renault Centre at Swindon in 1982 or Richard Rogers' single-storey factory buildings in France, dating from the same period. Schlumberger represents a decisive rupture with this approach in that, while its offices remain systematised and modular, the Teflon tent makes an independent statement, totally removed in its plasticity from the well-serviced anonymity of the High-Tech approach. Moreover Hopkins' decision to place the support structure outside the tent was at variance with the early Foster precept of always enclosing the structure within the membrane.

The Schlumberger tent structure consists of three boldly scalloped, balloon-like forms, suspended from tubular pylons and steel rods. These linked tents cover a two-bay, sunken test area devoted to drilling research and a one-bay winter-garden-cum-café terrace. Unlike the flatter, high-riding tents of Hopkins' Basildon proposal, Schlumberger assumes the appearance of a grounded dirigible, flanked on its eastern and western edges by a skirt of scientists' rooms and laboratories.

If one dates the emergence of a certain productivism in British architecture with Team 4's Reliance Controls factory built

at Swindon in 1967, then the so-called High-Tech movement is now around 25 years old, which is a long time for an approach to hold its own in a volatile age. The longevity of this line, both as a productive method and as a syntax, may perhaps be best appreciated if one compares its duration to the Dutch Neoplastic movement that lasted for barely 13 years. Seen in this light, the practice's current work assumes a transitional character, one in which the architects have gradually drawn away from the techno-ideology of the High-Tech movement in its prime.

This shift first became evident in the 1984 Hopkins design for the Mound Stand at Lord's Cricket Ground in London. Hopkins' response to the traditional context was to extend the brick-arched undercroft of the Frank Verity stand along the St John's Wood Road and to cover the new seating with an elevated superstructure, surmounted by a lightweight tent. This last element, seemingly combining the overtones of a village marquee with the British nautical tradition, was paradoxically derived from the lightweight suspension structures of Frei Otto. However, unlike the simplicity of the typical Otto tent, Hopkins' flying roof is hung from six tubular steel masts that pass through the brick-arched stadium to carry raked seating above. This structure also supports a trussed girder from which the dining level and the so-called hospitality seating are suspended. This truss also serves as a tie-back for the roof; it is the means by which any compressive upward wind load is transferred down through solid rods anchored to the brick undercroft. The structural character of this trussed transfer floor is expressed through horizontal steel panelling that stiffens the structure, while glass-block infill panels illuminate the private dining rooms beneath. The polyester roof hangs from the tubular masts as a catenary structure, cable-stayed into position. With each of the oculi let into the tent, the domed aperture is held open by spoked, pick-up rings and covered by clear polycarbonate bubbles.

The fact that the stand is used only in summer enabled the engineer, John Thornton of Ove Arup & Partners, to establish a clear differentiation between the *earthwork* of the public stand,

Left, Team 4: Reliance Controls, Swindon, 1967. Far left, Foster Associates: Hammersmith Broadway proposal for London Transport, 1978.

carried on brick arches, and the *roofwork* of the mast-supported tent with its cantilevered floor. The way in which these different tectonic conditions were able to appeal to different ideological and aesthetic constituencies, is no doubt responsible for the positive reception enjoyed by this building.

Given this interaction between old and new it is hardly surprising that the next commission – for the Solid State Logic company, erected in Begbroke village, near Oxford, in 1988 – would take Hopkins closer to the Structural Rationalism of Viollet-le-Duc and the work of Louis Kahn rather than to the neo-Miesianism that it superficially displays on its exterior. The proof of this lies in the absence of a suspended ceiling on the ground floor (such ceilings were anathema to Kahn) and its presence on the floor above, a schism that only serves to reinforce the transitional character of the work. The fact that the ground floor is mainly given over to the manufacture of recording and broadcasting equipment and that the upper floor is largely devoted to research and development, does little to account for the different approaches adopted towards servicing the space in each instance. In the case of the upper floor, the air supply and lighting are incorporated in a standard manner into the depth of a space frame, whereas on the ground floor the air is piped in and extracted centrally within a series of recessed lighting domes, ringed with concentric fluorescent lighting. By deciding to coffer an in-situ concrete floor and to suspend a lightweight elevated deck above it, Hopkins adopted a categorically critical attitude towards the received language of High-Tech architecture. In fact, by the mid 1980s, the Hopkins practice seemed to be moving in two directions simultaneously: on the one hand towards lightweight, suspended fabric construction; on the other, closer to the work of Pier Luigi Nervi, whose Gatti Wool Factory near Rome of 1954 can be said to point, however indirectly, to the concrete coffered floor of Solid State Logic.

In his first work for David Mellor at Hathersage in 1989, Hopkins followed his Mound Stand exercise in loadbearing brickwork with a bonded stone wall built on the circular foundations of an old gasholder. Playing with the industrial

Pier Luigi Nervi: Gatti Wool Works, near Rome, 1954.

vernacular of the region, Hopkins and Mellor rendered this factory as a 'round house', faced in machine-cut stone and roofed with self-bracing steel trusses. The tectonic emphasis in this instance falls on the roof structure. This is a built-up, tubular-steel truss roof held in place by a system of adjustable tie rods that restrain the foot of each truss. These feet define an expressive open 'cornice' situated just below the gutterless eaves of the building.

With the second commission for Mellor, a showroom and office building erected at Shad Thames in London, 1991, Hopkins adopted a tectonic that was categorically removed from both lightweight technology and vernacular form. The key in this instance was the decision to try for a building that, as in the work of Auguste Perret, would be an especially refined version of in-situ, fairfaced concrete construction. Mellor and Hopkins went to extraordinary lengths to produce a finish that was precise while preserving the moulded quality of the material. Thus the plywood formwork was ordered to a special size and two types of joints were devised, a recessed joint made by using special aluminium extrusions and a projecting joint formed by chamferring the edges of the plywood. The concrete was hand finished with glasspaper in order to give it a finish close to polished stone. The one other material that offset the tectonic quality of the concrete was the one that Kahn regarded as its alchemical opposite, namely lead, a material that Mellor and Hopkins had previously employed in the factory. It is significant, in this regard, that Hopkins worked on Mellor's Thameside building just after visiting Kahn's Mellon Center for British Art at Yale.

The late 1980s saw a change in the work of the Hopkins practice, which arose out of a number of mediating factors: on the one hand the scale and the number of commissions increased; on the other the methodology and the mode of expression began to vary over a wider range. The overall success of the Mound Stand was decisive, for it recommended itself as a hybrid approach, with which to reconcile the rather contradictory demands then prevailing in British society. Consciously or otherwise, the practice began to assume two

rather different expressive lines: firstly, a continuing hard-line commitment to technological rationality and, secondly, a more conciliatory approach to traditional modes of construction. While the neo-Miesian New Square office complex at Bedfont Lakes near Heathrow of 1992 may be regarded as representative of the first, the second method came to the fore with the realisation of Bracken House, first projected as a new building and then as the provision of similar accommodation within an existing structure.

The schizophrenic character of Solid State Logic – the split let us say between its concrete isostatic first-floor slab and its overall Miesian appearance, caused the partnership to approach the initial design for Bracken House in a fresh way, one in which a shallow, barrel-vaulted flooring system, made of in-situ concrete cast over permanent sheet steel formwork, was combined with concrete-filled tubular steel columns and welded steel plate girders, the whole jointly expressed on the exterior as an exposed steel skeleton frame. Of welded, plated steel construction throughout, Bracken House as originally designed was a ferro-vitreous hybrid, compounded, in part, of Georges Chedanne's *Parisien Libéré* building in the rue Réaumur, Paris of 1904 and in part of Franco Albini and Franca Helg's *La Rinascente* department store, completed in Rome in 1953. While Foster's building for Willis Faber & Dumas in Ipswich of 1975, on which Michael Hopkins had worked, also lay behind the sectional organisation of Bracken House, it was nonetheless a totally new departure, given the loadbearing stone piers carrying the load of the frame through metal-hinged bearings. This homage to Peter Behrens' AEG Turbine Factory in Berlin of 1910 also remains in Bracken House as built, although in this instance the stone piers are shorter and the bearing is more complicated.

Coming to terms with history

Bracken House compelled the Hopkins practice to confront history in a new way, in part because they had to reconstruct an existing building and, in part because they brought to this task a growing conviction that the late 20th century demanded a

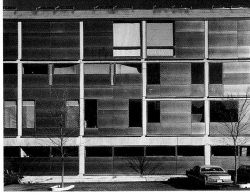

Top, David Mellor Offices and Showroom, Shad Thames, London, 1991. Bottom, Louis Kahn: Mellon Center for British Art at Yale, New Haven, USA, 1953. Right, Peter Behrens: the AEG Turbinenfabrik, Berlin, 1910.

reformulation of the contemporary architectural repertoire. As we have seen from the initial design, this caused them to reappraise French Structural Rationalism; the syntax that had played such a prominent role in the evolution of modern architecture from the Gothic Revival onwards. Thus Bracken House as realised openly evokes Peter Ellis' Oriel Chambers, completed in Liverpool in 1864, which, while hardly Gothic Revival is surely closely related, with its shallow brick-arched floors and its cast-iron bay-window frames. Indeed, the complexity of the structure in Bracken House took Hopkins' practice closer to the Gothic than Ellis himself, since the spread-eagled gunmetal brackets carrying the curtain wall had to be tied back by exposed steel tie rods anchored to the foundations, the whole attaining a level of thrust and counter thrust that would have been the envy of Viollet-le-Duc. The full resonance of Hopkins' intervention at Bracken House hardly ends here, however, for the glass block, light-shaft-cum-atrium, set in the centre of the doughnut plan, evokes a series of French precedents ranging from Henri Labrouste's book stacks in the Bibliothèque Nationale in Paris, to the Joachim Company's perfection of *le bêton translucide*, dating from 1911, as a system for building waterproof roofs and floors made of glass lenses set in concrete.[2]

The tectonic system broached by Bracken House, in its two incarnations, culminates in two inner-London projects of considered consequence. These may both be seen, as Hopkins suggests, as 'technology coming to town'; that is to say as a situation in which the High-Tech mode as employed in open countryside has been contextually modified in order to respond to the cultural fabric of the city. The two works in question are a perimeter block proposed for London Transport on the Tottenham Court Road tube station site and the New Parliamentary Building facing the Houses of Parliament in Bridge Street, Westminster.

The New Parliamentary Building, which like the Tottenham Court Road scheme is arranged as a perimeter block over rail lines, builds on the tectonic theme of Bracken House. The design develops the loadbearing stone pier, as a full-height,

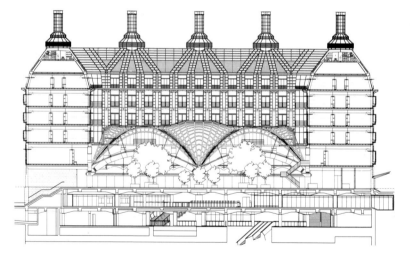

Right, Louis Kahn: Phillips Exeter Academy Library, New Haven, USA, 1972. Far right, New Parliamentary Building, Westminster, London, 1989–.

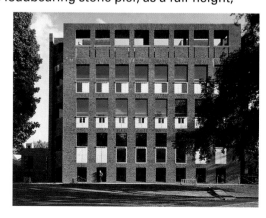

five-storey element, stepping out as it descends, to pick up consecutive floor loads. In this instance the loadbearing stone is restrained by a monolithic, reinforced concrete armature, running around all four sides of a lightcourt and comprising hollow shell vaults carried on reinforced concrete frames.

One of the most intriguing things about this design is the way in which it once again returns to the work of Kahn, above all to the loadbearing brick piers of the Phillips Exeter Academy Library, 1972, and the dialectic between the rising ventilation shafts and descending structure as this appears in Kahn's early sketches for the Richards Medical Laboratories of 1957. The New Parliamentary Building appears to synthesise these two tropes into a single paradigm. Here the vertical shafts of the laboratories are echoed by bronze ducts stepping out as they pass upwards between diminishing stone piers and vertical bay windows, eventually to bond back over the surface of a semi-mansard roof, like a manifold, radiating out every three bays from a central air-exhaust mounted on the roof. As if this weren't enough, this work also entertains the use of cable-reinforced, stone arches in order to transfer the loads of the piers around the perimeter of the lightcourt, thereby reducing the number of point loads to be carried over the underground railway beneath the building. One can hardly overestimate the audacious character of this distribution of point loads onto stone arches that span free over the lightcourt, with everything depending on cable-reinforced, precision-cut stone. This is a *tour de force* in which the flat arch is conceived as a series of hinges. The structural conception and calculation is once again the work of John Thornton of Ove Arup & Partners. Suddenly one finds oneself on a threshold where the former High-Tech quest for productive economy turns paradoxically into a surplus of sophisticated technique in which, budget permitting, one will turn the clock back not only to re-read history but also to scramble it!

Responding to an emerging ecological and cultural consensus, Michael Hopkins and Partners have striven over the last decade to expand their technical and syntactical repertoire so as to embrace heavyweight constructional forms with lower energy characteristics and geater durability. Following the tradition of hybrid construction extending from Henri Labrouste to Kahn, they have tried to reinforce and energise the massiveness of such forms with lightweight, relieving components of various kinds, from steel space frames to prestressed concrete beams, from cable suspension to post-tensioned stonework. As of now, this approach comes to its fullest realisation in the New Parliamentary Building, where the contextual response is such as to suggest a comparison with the work of Renzo Piano. Both practices appear to have the same ostensible aim, namely to inflect their production according to its context. Herein resides the main difference between them, for what is decisive in each case is the exact manner in which this inflection is achieved. In this regard one may observe distinct nuances of sensibility and method, for where the Hopkins practice will enter into the direct citation of traditional syntax – as with David Mellor's Hathersage factory or the Mound Stand – or will replicate, however subtly, the profiling of the urban context – as with the matching silhouettes of the New Parliamentary Building and New Scotland Yard – Piano's Building Workshop tends to achieve its traditional allusions through revetment, as with the local grey timber siding of the Menil Collection museum or in the terracotta tiles hung onto the cladding of their perimeter housing block, inserted into the rue de Meaux in Paris. In both instances there is a turn towards non-metallic, opaque construction as a primary expressive material, so much so that one senses that somewhere between these two post High-Tech positions there lies a subtle spectrum of techniques in which to ground the future of tectonic form.

1 *Architects' Journal*, 13.7.77 p374.
2 See Raymond McGrath and A C Frost, *Glass in Architecture and Decoration*, Architectural Press, London, 1937, pp268–9.

Louis Kahn: Richards Medical Laboratories, Philadelphia, USA, 1962.

Michael Hopkins and Partners

Partners

Michael Hopkins CBE, RA,
AADipl, RIBA
Born 1935.
Senior partner, Michael Hopkins
and Partners.
Founded firm in 1976

Patricia Hopkins AADipl
Born 1942.
Co-founder of Michael Hopkins
and Partners in 1976

John Pringle AADipl RIBA
Born 1951.
Joined Michael Hopkins & Partners
in 1978; partner since 1981

Ian Sharratt MA (RCA)
Born 1948.
Joined Michael Hopkins & Partners
in 1976; partner since 1981

William Taylor MA DipArch RIBA
Born 1957.
Joined Michael Hopkins and
Partners in 1982; partner since 1987

Associates

Peter Romaniuk BSc BArch
David Selby BA(Hons) DipArch RIBA
Robin Snell MA DipArch RIBA
James Greaves DipArch RIBA
Andrew Barnett MA DipArch RIBA

Chronology

● 1975–76
Hopkins House,
Hampstead, London
● 1976–77
Willis Faber & Dumas
London Headquarters,
Trinity Square, City of London
● 1977–80
Greene King Draught
Beer Cellars,
Bury St Edmunds
● 1978–79
IBM Sales Centre,
Birmingham
● 1979–80
Tube Investments
Headquarters Fit-out,
Mayfair, London
● 1979–81
Greene King Wine
and Spirits' Store,
Bury St Edmunds
● 1980–82
Patera Building System,
Stoke on Trent
● 1981–83
Greene King Golf Club House,
Milton Keynes
● 1981–84
IBM Education Centre,
St John's Wood, London
● 1981–
Basildon Town Centre,
Essex
● 1982–83
Research Machines Research
and Development Facilities,
Oxford
● 1982–85
Schlumberger Cambridge
Research Centre, Phase One,
Cambridge
● 1982–85
Willis Faber Computer
and Service Centre,
Ipswich
● 1983–85
Daily Telegraph Editorial
and Management Fit-out,
London Docklands
● 1984–85
Hopkins Office,
Marylebone, London
● 1984–86
Fleet Velmead Infants School,
Hampshire
● 1984–87
Mound Stand,
Lord's Cricket Ground,
Westminister, London
● 1986–88
Solid State Logic Development
and Production Building,
Begbroke, Oxford
● 1986–88
Victoria and Albert Museum
Masterplan and Galleries,
Kensington, London
● 1987–89
Jardines Headquarters Fit-out,
London

● 1987–91
Financial Times Editorial and
Management Fit-out,
Southwark, London
● 1987–92
Bracken House, City of London
● 1988–89
David Mellor Cutlery Factory,
Hathersage, Derbyshire
● 1988–
Savacentre Store,
Hedge End, Hampshire
● 1988–91
David Mellor Offices
and Showroom,
Shad Thames, London
● 1989–91
Compton and Edrich Stands,
Lord's Cricket Ground, London
● 1989–92
New Square, Bedfont Lakes,
Masterplan and Offices,
Heathrow, Middlesex
● 1989–
Marylebone Gate Office
Development,
Westminster, London
● 1989–94
Glyndebourne Opera House,
Glyndebourne, East Sussex
● 1989–
New Parliamentary Building,
Westminster, London
● 1990–
Younger Universe, Edinburgh
● 1990–
Tottenham Court Road
Station Redevelopment,
Westminster, London
● 1990–
Westminster Underground
Station Redevelopment,
London
● 1990–92
Schlumberger Cambridge
Research Centre, Phase Two,
Cambridge
● 1990–
Masterplan for Lord's
Cricket Ground,
Westminster, London
● 1991–
Victoria Transport Interchange,
Westminster, London
● 1992–93
Raphael Cartoon Gallery,
Victoria and Albert Museum
Kensington, London
● 1992–94
New Inland Revenue Centre,
Nottingham
● 1992–
Paddington Station
Masterplan, London
● 1993
Emmanuel College Lecture
Theatre Building,
Cambridge
● 1993–
Residential Home for
Jewish Care,
Finchley, London
● 1993–
Offices for News International,
Wapping, London

Credits: Buildings

**Hopkins House,
Hampstead, London 1975–1976**
Design team: Michael Hopkins,
Patricia Hopkins
Structural engineer:
Anthony Hunt Associates
● Awards: RIBA Awards for
Architecture 1977; Civic Trust
Award 1979

**Greene King Draught Beer Cellars,
Bury St Edmunds, Suffolk,
1977–1981**
Client: Greene King plc
Design team: Michael Hopkins,
John Pringle, Ian Sharratt,
David Harriss, Mark Sutcliffe,
Chris Wilkinson
Structural engineer:
Anthony Hunt Associates
Services engineer:
R.W. Gregory & Partners
Quantity surveyor:
Davis Belfield & Everest
Management contractor:
Bovis Construction Ltd
● Awards: RIBA Awards for
Architecture 1980; Structural Steel
Award 1980; Financial Times
Architecture Award 1980
(industrial award)

Patera Building System, 1980–1982
Client: Patera Products Ltd
Design team: Michael Hopkins,
John Pringle, Peter Romaniuk,
David Allsop, Chris Williamson
Structural engineer:
Anthony Hunt Associates
Services engineer:
Dale & Goldfinger
Fire engineering consultant:
Ove Arup & Partners

**Schlumberger Cambridge Research
Centre, Phase One, Cambridge,
1982–1985**
Client: Schlumberger Cambridge
Research Ltd
Design team: Michael Hopkins,
John Pringle, Chris Williamson,
Nic Bewick, Robin Snell, John Eger
Structural engineers:
Anthony Hunt Associates;
Ove Arup & Partners
(membrane & cables)
Services engineer:
YRM Engineers
Quantity surveyor:
Davis Belfield & Everest
Acoustic consultant:
Tim Smith Acoustics
Fire consultant:
Ove Arup & Partners
Main contractor: Bovis
Construction Ltd
● Awards: RIBA National Awards
for Architecture 1988; Civic Trust
Award 1988; Structural Steel Award
1988; Financial Times Architecture
Award 1985

**Fleet Velmead Infants School,
Fleet, Hampshire, 1984–1986**
Client: Hampshire County Council
Design team: Michael Hopkins,
Patricia Hopkins, Sheila Thompson,
Bill Dunster
Structural and services engineer:
Buro Happold
Quantity surveyor:
Davis Belfield & Everest
Main contractor:
Wates Construction (Southern)
● Awards: Structural Steel
Award 1988

**Mound Stand, Lord's Cricket
Ground, Westminster, London,
1984–1987**
Client: Marylebone Cricket Club
Design team: Michael Hopkins,
John Pringle, William Taylor,
David Selby, David Sparrow,
Andrew Barnett, Jee Seng Heng,
Ernest Fasanya, Bill Dunster,
Simon Herron, Adam Matthews,
Martin Hsu
Structural and services engineer:
Ove Arup & Partners
Fire consultant:
Ove Arup & Partners
Quantity surveyor:
Davis Belfield & Everest
Main contractor:
Higgs & Hill Management
Contracting Ltd
● Awards: RIBA National Awards
for Architecture 1988; Civic Trust
Award 1988

**Solid State Logic Development and
Production Building, Begbroke,
Oxfordshire, 1986–1988**
Client: Solid State Logic
Design team: Michael Hopkins,
Ian Sharratt, Peter Romaniuk,
Peter Cartwright, Bill Dunster,
Graham Saunders
Structural and services engineer:
Buro Happold
Quantity surveyor:
Davis Langdon & Everest
Main contractor:
Walter Lawrence Project
Management
● Awards: Financial Times
Architecture Award 1989 (finalist);
RIBA National Awards for
Architecture 1989; Civic Trust
Award 1990

Cutlery Factory for David Mellor, Hathersage, Derbyshire, 1988–1989
Client: David Mellor Design Ltd
Design team: Michael Hopkins, John Pringle, Bill Dunster, Neno Kezic
Structural engineer: Whitby and Bird
Main contractor: David Mellor Design Ltd
● Award: RIBA National Awards for Architecture 1989

David Mellor Offices and Showroom, Southwark, London, 1988–1991
Client: David Mellor Design Ltd
Design team: Michael Hopkins, John Pringle, Bill Dunster, Ernest Fasanya
Structural engineer: Buro Happold
Quantity surveyor: Pritchard Williams & Hunt
Main contractors: Sir Robert McAlpine Management Contracting Ltd (reinforced-concrete frame, including blockwork); David Mellor Design Ltd (other areas)

Compton and Edrich Stands, Lord's Cricket Ground, Westminster, London, 1989–1991
Client: Marylebone Cricket Club
Design team: Michael Hopkins, John Pringle, Ernest Fasanya, Emma Adams, Chris Thurlbourne
Structural and services engineer: Ove Arup & Partners
Fire consultant: Ove Arup & Partners
Quantity surveyor: Davis Langdon & Everest
Main contractor: John Lelliott (Contracts) Ltd
● Award: Concrete Society Awards 1992

New Square, Bedfont Lakes, Heathrow, Middlesex, 1989–1992
Client: MEPC/IBM Joint Venture
Design team: Michael Hopkins, Ian Sharratt, Peter Romaniuk, Pamela Bate, Peter Cartwright, Brendan Phelan, Jane Willoughby, Stephen Macbean, Gerhard Landau, Dominique Gagnon, Susan Hillberg, Marybeth McTeague, Andy Young, Chin Lai, Tommaso del Buono, John Hoepfner, Michael Wentworth, Danielle Mantelin, Clare Endicott
Structural and fire engineer: Buro Happold
Services engineer: FHP Partnership
Quantity surveyor: Bucknall Austin
Acoustic consultant: Moir Hands & Associates
Landscape consultant: Land Use Consultants
Planning consultant: Grimley J R Eve
Main contractor: Costain Construction Ltd

Bracken House, City of London, 1987–1992
Client: Obayashi Europe BV
Design team: Michael Hopkins, John Pringle, David Selby, Robin Snell, Bill Dunster, Arif Mehmood, Patrick Nee, Andrew Barnett, Helena Webster, Emma Nsugbe, Alessando Calafati, Ernest Fasanya, Emma Adams, Loretta Gentilini, Maki Kuwayama, Mike Eleftheriades, Colin Muir, Neno Kezic, Tommaso del Buono, Steve Piponides, Nicholas Boyarsky, Gail Halvorsen, Amir Sanei, Robert Bishop, Fiona Thompson, Eva Jensen, Margaret Leong, Nick Malby, Pippa Nissen, Joao Passanha, Oriel Prizeman, Sundeep Singh Bhamra, Ameer Bin Tahir, Chris Thurlbourne, Jim Dunster, Boon Yang Sim, Charles Webster, Sanja Polescuk, Gina Raimi
Structural and services engineer: Ove Arup & Partners
Quantity surveyor: Northcroft Neighbour & Nicholson
Construction consultant: Schal International Ltd
Fire consultant: Arup Research & Development
Acoustic consultant: Arup Acoustics
Main contractor: Trollope and Colls Construction Ltd
● Awards: RIBA National Awards for Architecture 1992; British Construction Industry Award 1992

Schlumberger Cambridge Research Centre, Phase Two, Cambridge, 1990–1992
Client: Schlumberger Cambridge Research Ltd
Design team: Michael Hopkins, John Pringle, James Greaves, Alan Jones, Annabel Hollick
Structural and services engineer: Buro Happold
Quantity surveyor: Davis Langdon & Everest
Main contractor: Team Management (Southern) Ltd

Projects

Basildon Town Centre, Essex, 1981–
Client: Basildon Development Corporation
Design team: Michael Hopkins, John Pringle, William Taylor, Peter Romaniuk, David Sparrow, Andrew Barnett
Structural engineers: Buro Happold (superstructure); Basildon Development Corporation (substructure)
Services engineer: Buro Happold
Fire consultant: Ove Arup & Partners
Quantity surveyor: E.C. Harriss & Partners

Glyndebourne Opera House, East Sussex, 1988–1994
Client: Glyndebourne Productions Ltd
Design team: Michael Hopkins, Patricia Hopkins, John Pringle, Robin Snell, Andrew Barnett, Arif Mehmood, Pamela Bate, Peter Cartwright, Justin Bere, Andrew Wells, Lucy Lavers, Edward Williams, Martin Pease, Emma Nsugbe, Nigel Curry, Loretta Gentilini, Jim Dunster, Tommaso del Buono, Kevin O'Sullivan, Marc Turkel, Margaret Mitchell, Julie Hamilton
Structural and services engineer: Ove Arup & Partners
Quantity surveyor: Gardiner & Theobald
Acoustic consultant: Arup Acoustics
Lighting consultant: George Sexton Associates
Main contractor: Bovis Construction Ltd

New Parliamentary Building, Westminster, London, 1989–
Client: Parliamentary Works Directorate
Design team: Michael Hopkins, John Pringle, David Selby, Bill Dunster, Emma Adams, Michael Taylor, Chris Bannister, Gail Halvorsen, Margaret Leong, Robert Bishop, Amir Sanei, Alexandra Small, Gina Raimi, Buddy Haward
Structural and services engineer: Ove Arup & Partners
Quantity surveyor: Gardiner & Theobald
Acoustic consultant: Arup Acoustics
Fire consultant: Arup Research & Development
Lighting consultant: Lichtplanung Christian Bartenbach

Marylebone Gate Office Development, Westminster, London, 1989–
Client: Lynton plc
Design team: Michael Hopkins, William Taylor, James Greaves, Alan Jones, Ben Fereday, Lydia Haack, Melody Mason, Justin Bere, William Lee, Kit Man Leong, Sarah Parker
Structural and services engineer: Ove Arup & Partners
Quantity surveyor: WT Partnership

Westminster Underground Station Redevelopment, London, 1990–
Client: London Underground Ltd
Design team: Michael Hopkins, John Pringle, David Selby, Patrick Nee, Gordon McKenzie, Emma Adams, Ian Milne, Gail Halvorsen, Annabel Hollick, Georgina Hall, Geoff Whittaker, Amir Sanei, Alexandra Small, Gina Raimi
Structural and services engineer:
Civil engineer: G Maunsell & Partners
Quantity surveyor: Gardiner & Theobald
Acoustic consultant: Arup Acoustics
Fire consultant: Arup Research & Development
Lighting consultant: George Sexton Associates

Tottenham Court Road Station Redevelopment, Westminster, London, 1990–
Client: London Regional Transport
Design team: Michael Hopkins, William Taylor, James Greaves, Ben Fereday, Simon Fraser, Lydia Haack, Georgina Hall, Julie Hamilton
Structural and services engineer: Ove Arup & Partners
Quantity surveyor: Cyril Sweet & Partners

Tottenham Court Road Station Ticket Hall, Westminster, London, 1990–
Client: London Underground Ltd
Design team: Michael Hopkins, William Taylor, Patrick Nee, Emma Nsugbe, Russell Baylis, Maureen Stovell
Structural and services engineers: Ove Arup & Partners; London Underground Ltd
Quantity surveyor: Franklin & Andrews

Younger Universe, Edinburgh, 1990–
Clients: Holyrood Brewery Foundation with Lothian & Edinburgh Enterprise Ltd
Design team: Michael Hopkins, Ian Sharratt, Jane Willoughby, Andrew Young, Ernest Sim Fasanya, Justin Bere, Carol Painter
Structural and services engineer: Ove Arup & Partners
Quantity surveyor: Gardiner & Theobald
Main contractor: Team Management (Scotland) Ltd

Victoria Transport Interchange, Westminster, London, 1991–
Client: Greycoats London Estates
Design team: Michael Hopkins, Ian Sharratt, William Taylor, Ernest Sim Fasanya, Jane Willoughby, Catherine Martin, Mike Wentworth, Gerhard Landau, Carol Painter
Structural and services engineer: Ove Arup & Partners
Acoustic consultant: Arup Acoustics
Construction consultant: Schal International Ltd
Quantity surveyor: Davis Langdon & Everest
Planning consultant: Rolfe Judd

New Inland Revenue Centre, Nottingham, 1992–1994
Client: Inland Revenue
Design team: Michael Hopkins, Ian Sharratt, William Taylor, Peter Romaniuk, Pamela Bate, Brendan Phelan, Stephen Macbean, Ernest Sim Fasanya, Brian Reynolds, Catherine Martin, Charles Walker, Guni Suri, Lynn Bacher, Jonathan Knight, Nathan Barr, Jason Cooper, Lydia Haack, Max Connop, Russell Baylis, Paul Cutler, Simon Fraser, Carol Painter
Structural and services engineer: Ove Arup & Partners
Quantity surveyor: Turner and Townsend Chartered Quantity Surveyors
Project management: Turner and Townsend Project Management
Lighting consultant: Lichtplanung Christian Bartenbach
Main contractor: Laing Management Ltd

Select bibliography

General
● *A Vision of Britain*,
HRH the Prince of Wales
(Doubleday, 1989)
● *Abitare*, 'London: eight architects,
eight styles', Jonathan Glancey,
March 1991
● *Architectural Review*, 'Hopkins
Rules', Colin Davies, May 1984
● *Building*, 'Hi-Tec Hopkins',
Martin Pawley, 5.6.92
● *Building Design*, 'Once More with
Feeling', Kester Rattenbury, 17.1.92
● *Building Design*, 'Great Architects
I Have Met', Jose Manser, 24.1.92
● *Country Life*, 'Beyond High-Tech',
Kenneth Powell, 17.11.88
● *Independent*, 'The Acceptable
Face of Modernism',
Roger Berthoud, 8.11.89
● *Independent on Sunday*, 'A Recent
Elevation', Tanya Harrod, 1.11.92
● *Spectator*, 'Far Pavilions',
Gavin Stamp, 14.9.91
● *Times*, 'New Designs on National
Treasures', Marcus Binney, 4.3.92

Hopkins House
● *Architects' Journal*,
'Glass House in Hampstead',
Deyan Sudjic, 13.7.77
● *Architects' Journal*,
'1977: Michael Hopkins',
Martin Pawley, 16.10.85
● *Architectural Review*,
'House in Hampstead',
John Winter, December 1977
● *RIBA Journal*, 'Architect's Own
House', August 1977
● *RIBA Yearbook 1980*,
'London Now', Christopher Gotch

Greene King Draught Beer Cellars
● *Architectural Review*, 'Racking in
Suffolk', John Winter, March 1981

Patera Building System
● *Architects' Journal*, 'Patera as
Process', John Worthington,
'Fabrication and Erection', John
Pringle and John Winter, 'Patera as
Product', John Winter, 1.9.82
● *Architectural Review*, 'Preview
'82', Lance Knobel, January 1982

**Schlumberger Cambridge
Research Centre**
● *Architects' Journal*, 'Hopkins at
Cambridge', Birkin Haward, 1.2.84
● *Architects' Journal*, 'High Flyer',
Henry Herzberg, 24.10.84
● *Architects' Journal*, 'A Glimpse of
Tomorrow', Patrick Hannay, 15.5.85
● *Architects' Journal*, 'A Cambridge
Test: Hopkins for Schlumberger',
Steven Groak, 18.9.85
● *Architects' Journal*, 'Technology
Stretching High-Tech', John Winter
and Sarah Jackson, 28.10.92

Fleet Velmead Infants School
● *Architects' Journal*, 'Setting Sail
at Fleet: Velmead Infants School',
Patrick Hannay, 30.9.87

**The Mound Stand,
Lord's Cricket Ground**
● *The Mound Stand:
Lord's Cricket Ground*,
David Jenkins (Phaidon, 1991)
● *Architects' Journal*, 'Fit for the
Test: the Mound Stand, Lord's',
John Winter, 2.9.87
● *Architectural Review*, 'Cricket
Stand, Marylebone, London',
Peter Davey, September 1987

Solid State Logic
● *Architects' Journal*, 'Pavilion in
the Park: Solid State Logic HQ',
Colin Davies, 26.10.88

David Mellor Cutlery Factory
● *Abitare*, May 1991
● *Abitare*, December 1990
● *Architects' Journal*, 'Rounded
Design', Dan Cruickshank, 14.9.88
● *RIBA Journal*, 'Designing at the
Cutting Edge', Kenneth Murta,
October 1988

**David Mellor Offices and
Showroom**
● *Architectural Review*,
'Construction Celebration',
Colin Davies, October 1991
● *Designer's Journal*,
'Material Matters', Liz Hoggard,
October 1991

New Square, Bedfont Lakes
● *Architectural Review*, 'Bedfont
Duality', Colin Davies, October 1992
● *Building*, 'Parking at the
Crossroads', Martin Spring, 1.6.90
● *Building*, 'Lake Superior', Martin
Spring, 31.7.92
● *Building Design* (business parks'
supplement), 'Complementary
Coexistence', Jeremy Melvin,
July 1990

Bracken House
● *Bracken House*, Colin Amery
(Wordsearch Publishing, 1992)
● *Architects' Journal*, 'Inside Job:
Bracken House', John Winter,
27.5.92
● *Architects' Journal*, 'Changing
Times', Dan Cruickshank, 20.5.92
● *Architectural Review*, 'Gothic
Phoenix, Classic Support?',
Patrick Hodgkinson, May 1992

Index